THE Pointless Book

BUMPER EDITION

BLINK
bringing you closer

PUBLISHED BY BLINK PUBLISHING
3.25, THE PLAZA,
535 KING'S ROAD,
CHELSEA HARBOUR
LONDON, SW10 0SZ

WWW.BLINKPUBLISHING.CO.UK

FACEBOOK.COM/BLINKPUBLISHING
TWITTER.COM/BLINKPUBLISHING

978-1-910536-91-9

A CIP CATALOGUE OF THIS BOOK IS AVAILABLE FROM THE BRITISH LIBRARY.

DESIGN BY EMILY ROUGH, BLINK PUBLISHING

PRINTED AND BOUND BY GGP MEDIA GMBH, PÖßNECK

1 3 5 7 9 10 8 6 4 2

BLINK PUBLISHING IS AN IMPRINT OF THE BONNIER PUBLISHING GROUP
WWW.BONNIERPUBLISHING.CO.UK

THE POINTLESS BOOKS
APPS

CRANK UP THE POINTLESSNESS WITH THE POINTLESS BOOKS APPS AND DOWNLOAD EXCLUSIVE VIDEOS OF ALFIE! ACCESS THE FREE APPS FROM ITUNES OR GOOGLE PLAY, POINT YOUR DEVICE AT THE PAGES THAT DISPLAY THE SPECIAL POINTLESS 1 OR POINTLESS 2 ICONS AND THE VIDEOS WILL BE REVEALED ON SCREEN. MAKE SURE YOU OPEN THE CORRECT APP AND SCAN THE RIGHT PAGES!

HERE YOU WILL GET THE CHANCE TO WATCH VIDEOS OF ALFIE PLAYING HANDSLAPS, BAKING FULL ENGLISH CUPCAKES, DRAWING BLINDFOLDED AND, OF COURSE, MAKING A CAKE IN A MUG! THE POINTLESS BOOK 2 APP ALSO INCLUDES AUGMENTED REALITY TECHNOLOGY, ALLOWING YOU TO SHOW OFF YOUR CREATIVITY BY DESIGNING YOUR OWN POINTLESS CUP, BALL AND TRAINER! YOU CAN ALSO TAKE YOUR OWN PHOTOS WITH ALFIE AND SHARE THEM IN THE POINTLESS SELFIE BOOTH!

THE POINTLESS APPS REQUIRE AN INTERNET CONNECTION TO BE DOWNLOADED AND CAN BE USED ON IPHONE, IPAD OR ANDROID DEVICES. FOR DIRECT LINKS TO DOWNLOAD THE APP AND FOR FURTHER INFORMATION, VISIT WWW.BLINKPUBLISHING.CO.UK.

COMPLETE THIS BOOK IN A POINTLESS ORDER!

MY JOURNAL THIS WEEK

WEEK STARTING ___/___/___

WRITE DOWN ONE SENTENCE TO DESCRIBE EACH OF YOUR DAYS THIS WEEK.

MONDAY _____

_____

TUESDAY _____

_____

WEDNESDAY _____

_____

THURSDAY _____

_____

FRIDAY _____

_____

SATURDAY _____

_____

SUNDAY _____

_____

STICK A PHOTO HERE

WRITE DOWN YOUR FAVOURITE QUOTE AND WHO SAID IT

SEE
ALFIE'S
QUOTE

PB1

SPRAY YOUR FAVOURITE SCENT ON THIS PAGE FOR WHEN YOU'RE FEELING DOWN

SMELL ME

WOULD YOU RATHER...

SEE ALFIE'S CHOICES ⬤ PB1

1) Have wings or fins?

2) Have sweets for dinner every day for a month or have a pint of curdled milk?

3) Have no elbows or no knees?

4) Be in a cave of spiders or snakes?

5) Swim with crocodiles or sharks?

6) Drink your own urine or eat your own vomit?

7) Fight a horse-sized duck or 100 duck-sized horses?

8) Have legs as long as your fingers or fingers as long as your legs?

9) Be sexually attracted to fruit or have Cheetos dust permanently stuck to your fingers?

10) Speak any language fluently or be able to speak to animals?

WRITE DOWN YOUR TOP FIVE CELEBRITY CRUSHES

(LOOK AT THIS LIST A MONTH FROM NOW AND SEE IF YOU STILL AGREE!)

1.

2.

3.

4.

5.

ORIGAMI TIME!

CUT OUT THIS SQUARE AND FOLLOW THE
INSTRUCTIONS ON THE NEXT PAGE

CUT HERE

CUT HERE

CUT HERE

ORIGAMI TIME!

INSTRUCTIONS:

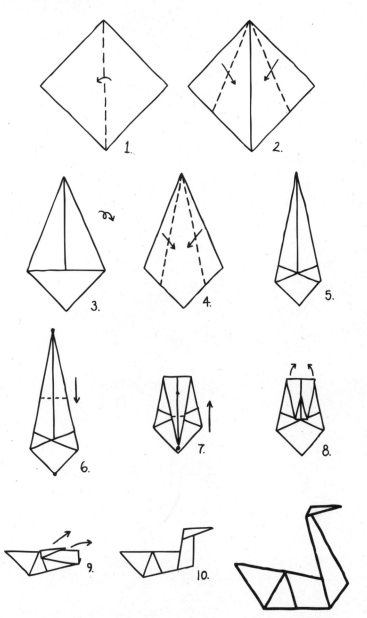

MAKE A PICTURE...

...WITH THE CIRCLE

BUCKET LIST

WRITE DOWN TEN THINGS YOU'D LIKE TO DO BEFORE YOU GET OLD...

1. GO TO PORTUGAL

2. HAVE A PET LAMB I SHEEP

3. CATCH A MARLIN

4. GO TO CUBA

~~5. SELL A MAGAZINE~~ MEET TOBI /TBJ2L

6. MEET OLIVERWHITE / OLI WHITE

7. MEET ALFIE DEYES / POINTLESSBLOG

8. MEET CHRIS MD / CHRIS

9. MEET MINI MINTER / SIMON

10. MEET JJ / KSI

TAKE YOUR POINTLESS BOOK ON A DATE...

WHERE DID YOU GO?

_____

_____

_____

_____

_____

WHAT DID YOU TALK ABOUT?

_____

_____

_____

_____

DID YOU KISS?

_____

_____

_____

ACCENTS CHALLENGE

Play the accents challenge with a few friends! Do your best impression of someone talking in the following accents and ask your friends to guess the country:

AUSTRALIAN

JAMAICAN

AMERICAN

FRENCH

CHINESE

SCOTTISH

POINTLESS PAGE!

WHEN YOU SEE THIS PAGE FILL IT IN WITH WHATEVER YOU WANT!

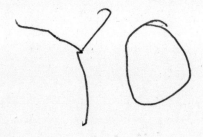

DRAW THE HAIR!

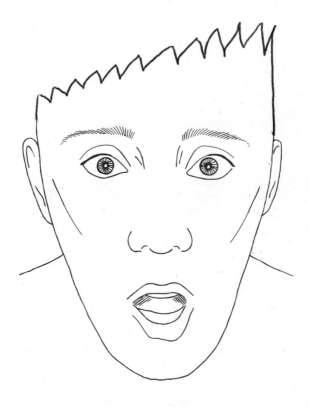

DRAW THE HAT!

DRAW SOME MAKE UP...

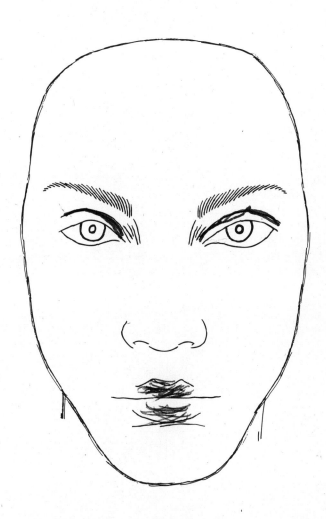

SPOT THE DIFFERENCE...

...FIVE DIFFERENCES TO FIND!

BRIGHTON PIER

DREAM JOURNAL

LAST NIGHT I DREAMT: _____

_____

_____

_____

_____

_____

_____

_____

_____

_____

_____

_____

_____

_____

_____

_____

_____

_____

I THINK THIS MEANS: _____

_____

_____

_____

_____

_____

_____

WRITE A MESSAGE FOR A FRIEND AND SWAP PAGES WITH THEM...

TEAR HERE

TAKE A BITE OUT
OF THIS PAGE

FAVOURITE EVER...

(LOOK BACK IN A MONTH AND UPDATE!)

BOOK: The diary of a wimpy kid

SONG: I LOVE CH1H

COLOUR: BLUE

YOUTUBER: CHris MD 1500

FRIEND: Will C

BLOGGER:

VIDEO GAME: /

FILM: /

WEBSITE: /

EAT SOME DRY CRACKERS...

HOW MANY CAN YOU GET IN YOUR
MOUTH AT ONCE?

_2_

HOW FAST CAN YOU EAT ONE
CRACKER?

_0'.28_

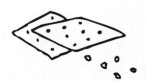

THE DICE GAME

CUT OUT THE PAPER CUBE TEMPLATE ON THE OPPOSITE
PAGE, FOLD ON THE LINES AND TAPE TOGETHER TO MAKE
THE DICE!

WRITE DOWN SIX THINGS THAT YOU **HAVE** TO DO IF YOU
ROLL THE DICE ON THAT NUMBER. IT CAN BE A DARE, A GOOD
DEED, ANYTHING, BUT YOU HAVE TO DO IT!

CUT OUT THE DICE TEMPLATE
(JUST THE OUTLINE)

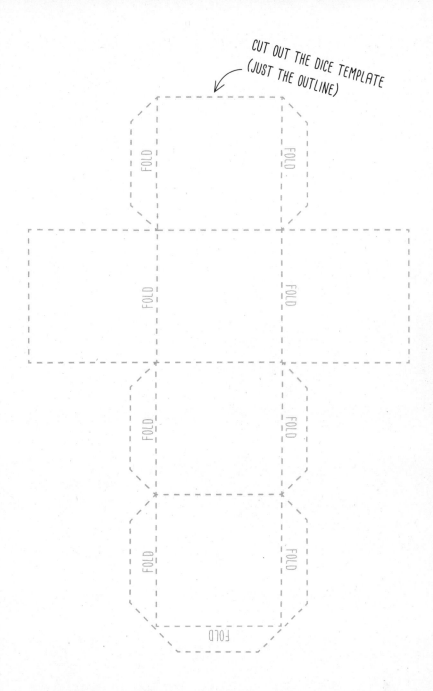

(YOU WILL NEED STICKY TAPE!)

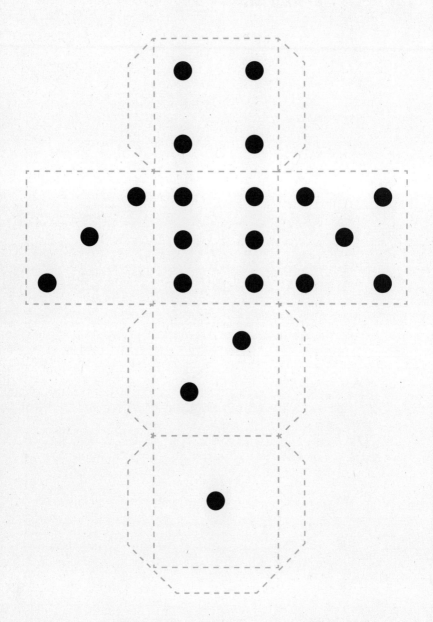

PLAY HAND-SLAPS

SCAN HERE

PB1

KEEP SCORE HERE:

PLAYER 1	PLAYER 2

WINNER: _____

DESIGN A TATTOO

DRAW A TATTOO YOU'D LOVE TO GET IN THE FUTURE

STAPLE THIS PAGE

CREATE SOME ART
#THEPOINTLESSBOOK
WITH YOUR DESIGN

PEOPLE-WATCHING PAGE...

TICK WHEN YOU SEE:

☑ A MAN WITH A BEARD

☑ A LADY WITH RED HAIR

☑ SOMEONE WEARING A CAST

☑ A CHILD WITH A DUMMY

☑ A YELLOW CAR

☑ SOMEONE TAKING A SELFIE

☑ A POSTMAN

DRAW THESE SHAPES...

...WITHOUT TAKING YOUR
PEN OFF THE PAPER

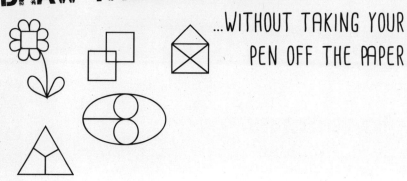

CONSEQUENCES...

FOLD HERE

...INSTRUCTIONS OVERLEAF

CONSEQUENCES...

PLAY WITH A FRIEND!

1. WRITE DOWN A GIRL'S NAME, FOLD IT OVER AND HAND TO THE NEXT PLAYER.

2. WRITE A BOY'S NAME, FOLD IT OVER AND PASS ON AGAIN.

3. WRITE WHERE THEY MET, FOLD OVER AND PASS ON.

4. WRITE WHAT SHE SAID TO HIM, FOLD OVER AND PASS ON.

5. WRITE WHAT HE SAID TO HER.

6. CONSEQUENCE...YOU DECIDE THE ENDING.

7. UNRAVEL THE STORY AND READ BACK!

WRITE DOWN YOUR FIVE FAVOURITE THINGS ABOUT YOURSELF AND WHY...

1.

2.

3.

4.

5.

PASS YOUR BOOK TO A STRANGER AND ASK THEM TO DRAW A PICTURE OF YOU...

WORD SEARCH!

B	O	Y	O	U	T	U	B	E	A	P	T	A	Q	R
F	I	R	B	V	B	T	S	X	H	C	B	C	H	P
O	N	D	V	J	R	S	E	W	P	O	H	S	G	O
T	K	J	K	G	M	K	W	N	Y	F	K	K	P	I
R	S	N	T	I	J	Y	S	D	R	F	C	V	S	N
A	M	J	L	Y	N	T	V	R	M	E	R	J	B	T
V	G	E	L	P	R	I	E	H	B	E	T	J	R	L
E	R	L	G	L	M	G	T	N	Q	Z	D	N	B	E
L	V	S	X	U	G	C	U	S	R	T	Z	K	I	S
E	D	U	T	O	W	F	B	Y	D	E	W	E	C	S
M	O	V	L	S	Z	G	T	H	I	U	L	U	F	B
L	N	V	O	P	L	H	B	R	E	F	Y	H	R	O
D	C	S	G	N	I	W	N	E	K	C	I	H	C	O
T	H	T	P	O	C	D	G	W	N	F	C	K	O	K
B	R	I	G	H	T	O	N	X	S	S	F	N	Y	S

YOUTUBE	SMILE	COFFEE
VLOGGER	BRIGHTON	INTERNET
POINTLESS BOOK	TRAVEL	CHICKEN WINGS

TRACE THE OUTLINE OF YOUR FAVOURITE FOOD ON THIS PAGE...

CONCERTINA STORY

WRITE A COUPLE OF LINES OF A STORY, FOLD BACK THE PAGE FOR A FRIEND TO
WRITE THE NEXT LINE AND SO ON... OPEN UP TO REVEAL A HILARIOUS STORY

FOLD HERE

...IRON THE CREASES OUT OF THIS PAGE.

PLAY A SONG AND WRITE THE LYRICS ON THIS PAGE...

DRAW GENITALS ON THE PEOPLE BELOW...

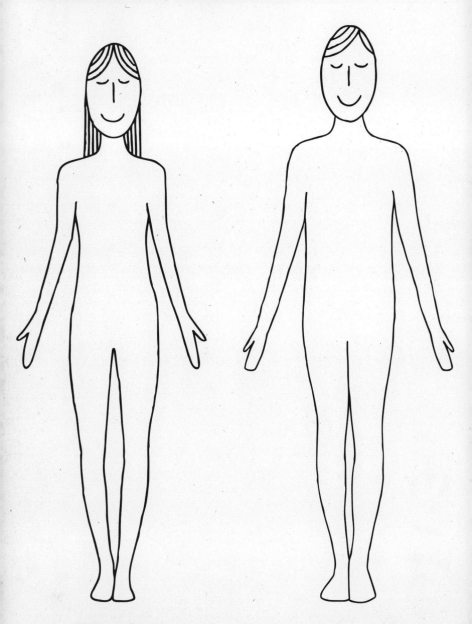

WRITE A COMPLIMENT ON THIS PAGE, RIP IT OUT AND PASS IT TO A FRIEND

TAKE A PHOTO OF YOURSELF HOLDING YOUR
BOOK IN THE CRAZIEST PLACE YOU CAN
THINK OF AND UPLOAD IT USING

#THEPOINTLESSBOOK

MAKE THIS PAGE AS MESSY AS YOU CAN

ALFIE'S CAKE IN A MUG RECIPE...

WATCH
ALFIE IN
ACTION

● PB1

INGREDIENTS

4 TBSP SELF-RAISING FLOUR

2 TBSP COCOA POWDER

4 TBSP CASTER SUGAR

3 TBSP MILK

1 MEDIUM EGG

3 TBSP VEGETABLE/
SUNFLOWER OIL

A FEW DROPS VANILLA
ESSENCE (IF YOU'RE
FEELING POSH)

2 TBSP CHOCOLATE CHIPS

METHOD

FIND A MUG. MAKE SURE IT'S A BIG ONE OTHERWISE IT'LL OVERFLOW IN THE MICROWAVE. PLUS WE ALL LIKE A BIG CAKE

THEN GET ALL THE INGREDIENTS OUT THE CUPBOARD AND READY. ADD THE FLOUR, COCOA POWDER AND SUGAR TO THE MUG AND MIX INTO A CHOCOLATY PASTE. ADD THE EGG AND GIVE IT A GOOD MIX; THEN ADD EVERYTHING ELSE - SO THE MILK, VEGETABLE OIL AND THE VANILLA ESSENCE - BUT NOT THE CHOCOLATE CHIPS! ONCE YOU HAVE EVERYTHING IN THE MUG AND IT'S LOOKING SMOOTH AND DELICIOUS ADD THE CHOCOLATE CHIPS.

PLACE YOUR LOVELY MUG IN THE MIDDLE OF THE MICROWAVE AND COOK ON THE HIGHEST SETTING FOR 4-5 MINUTES. KEEP AN EYE ON IT THROUGH THE WINDOW AS IT MIGHT OVERFLOW.

WAIT FOR THE 'DING'. THEN SIT DOWN AND EAT!

REMEMBER TO DRINK LOTS OF WATER TODAY. STAY HYDRATED :)

WRITE WHATEVER'S ON YOUR MIND

...WITHOUT STOPPING UNTIL YOU GET TO THE END OF THE PAGE

DRAW YOUR OWN TIME MACHINE

DRAW WHERE YOU'D LIKE TO GO - TO THE PAST OR THE FUTURE?

POINTLESS PAGE!

WHEN YOU SEE THIS PAGE FILL IT IN WITH WHATEVER YOU WANT!

A TEAR-OFF LETTER

WRITE SOMEONE YOU KNOW A LETTER ON THIS
PIECE OF PAPER, TEAR IT OFF AND SEND IT TO THEM

TEAR HERE

DOT TO DOT!

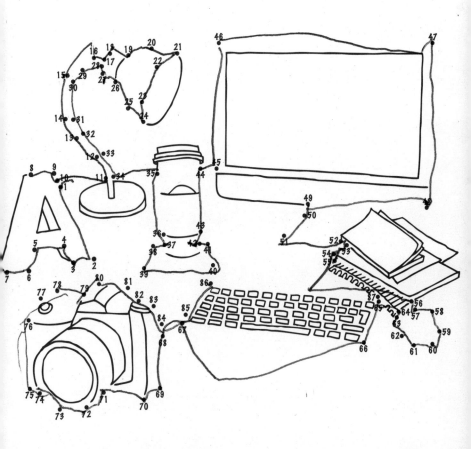

BURY THIS BOOK UNDERGROUND

(FOR ONE NIGHT, DIG IT UP AND SIGN THIS PAGE ONCE YOU'VE DONE SO.)

DATE: _____

SIGN HERE: _____

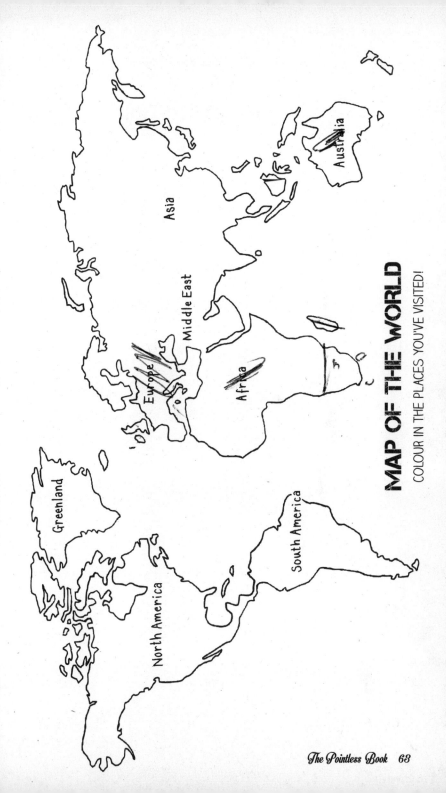

MAP OF THE WORLD

COLOUR IN THE PLACES YOU'VE VISITED!

Greenland

North America

South America

Asia

Middle East

Europe

Africa

Australia

MY LIFE AMBITIONS...

IN MY LIFE I WOULD LIKE TO...

1.

2.

3.

4.

5.

6.

PAPER AIRPLANE COMPETITION

RIP OUT THIS PAGE AND MAKE A PAPER AIRPLANE.

TEAR OUT

② FOLD

② FOLD

① FOLD

TEAR OUT

FOLD ③

FOLD ③

FOLD ⑤

FOLD ⑤

FOLD ④

FIVE YOGA POSITIONS TO LEARN...

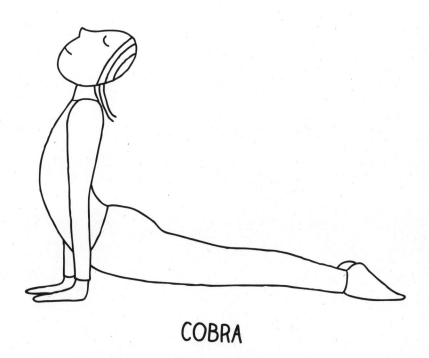

COBRA

FIVE YOGA POSITIONS TO LEARN...

DOWNWARD-FACING DOG

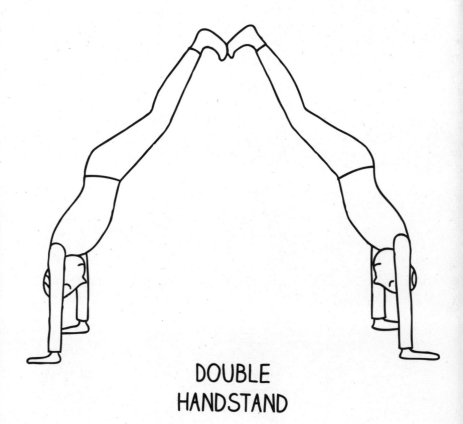

DOUBLE
HANDSTAND

FIVE YOGA POSITIONS TO LEARN...

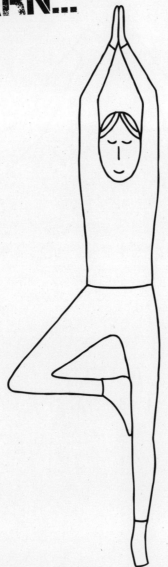

TREE

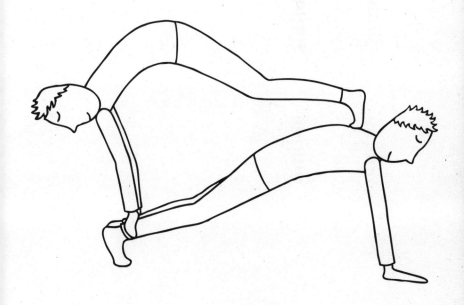

DOUBLE
TRIANGLE

GO TO PAGE 97

MESSAGE IN A BOOK...

WRITE A MESSAGE ON THIS PAGE, RIP IT OUT AND SNEAK IT INTO ANOTHER BOOK IN SCHOOL OR IN THE LIBRARY

TEAR HERE

IF YOU'RE LUCKY ENOUGH TO FIND THIS PAGE TWEET
#THEPOINTLESSBOOK

#THEPOINTLESSBOOK

DRAW A FINGER SELFIE...

PLACE A FINGER IN ONE OF THE SPACES BELOW AND DRAW A FACE, A BEARD, A CRAZY MOUSTACHE, WHATEVER YOU LIKE AND THERE YOU GO - YOU HAVE A FINGER SELFIE! SHARE YOUR FINGER SELFIES BY POSTING WITH #PBFINGERSELFIE

PLACES I'D LIKE TO TRAVEL TO...

PLAY SQUARES...

...WITH A FRIEND. TAKE TURNS MAKING A LINE JOINING TWO DOTS BUT TRY TO PREVENT THE OTHER PLAYER FROM MAKING A SQUARE. FILL THE DOTS WITH SQUARES AND THE PERSON WITH THE MOST WINS!

MY FAVOURITE CHILDHOOD MEMORY IS...

SEE
ALFIE'S
MEMORY

PB1

GRAFFITI THIS WALL

TURN THIS PAGE WITH YOUR ELBOW

WHAT IS THE LAST THING YOU DO BEFORE YOU FALL ASLEEP AND WHY?

TURN THIS PAGE WITH YOUR EAR

FLICK SOME PAINT ON THIS PAGE

FINISH OFF THE PICTURE...

NOT TO DO LIST...

WRITE DOWN FIVE THINGS YOU'D LIKE TO AVOID DOING TODAY:

1.

2.

3.

4.

5.

WRITE DOWN A SECRET...

ROAD TRIP!

First one to see a:...

RED CAR ☐

SERVICE STATION ☐

CROW ☐

TYRE ON THE SIDE OF THE ROAD ☐

GIRL WITH BLONDE HAIR ☐

GUY WEARING A BLUE T-SHIRT ☐

HITCHHIKER ☐

SEAGULL ☐

ROAD KILL ☐

BURGER VAN ☐

THE HEADBAND CHALLENGE

Rip out and write down the name of a famous person on the strips below. You and a mate lick and stick it on your head (don't look!) and each person asks a 'yes' or 'no' question in order to guess who their person is.

TEAR HERE

TEAR HERE

TEAR HERE

TEAR HERE

TEAR HERE

TEAR HERE

TEAR HERE

DO SOMETHING YOU'VE NEVER DONE BEFORE AND WRITE IT DOWN HERE.

DRAW YOUR DAY IN A STORYBOARD

DRAW HERE

WRITE HERE

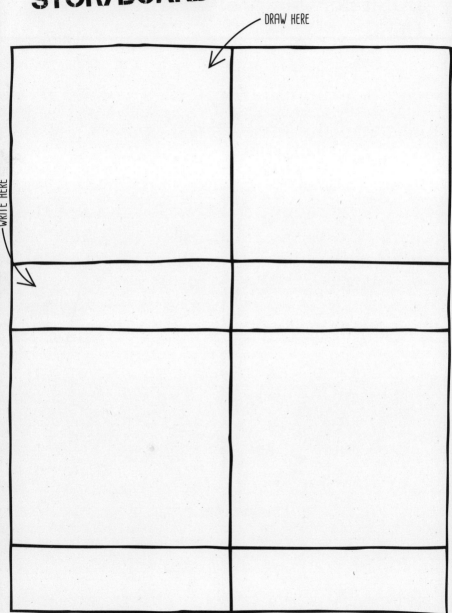

PASS THIS BOOK...

...WITH A GROUP OF FRIENDS
PASS THE BOOK UNDER YOUR
CHIN, WHOEVER DROPS IT IS OUT!

CHALLENGE TIME

OK, LET'S SEE HOW LONG YOU CAN BE SILENT FOR...

ATTEMPT 1: _____

ATTEMPT 2: _____

ATTEMPT 3: _____

ATTEMPT 4: _____

ATTEMPT 5: _____

PERSONAL BEST: _____

PRESS SOME FLOWERS...

...BETWEEN THESE PAGES

PAINT A PICTURE USING ONLY YOUR FINGERS...

LOVE LETTER...

...TEAR THIS PAGE OUT AND WRITE SOMEONE A
LOVE LETTER

TEAR HERE

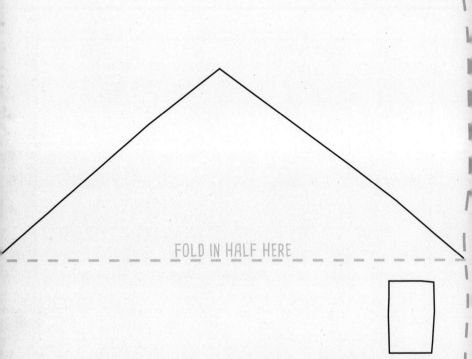

FOLD IN HALF HERE

PHONE BINGO!

Play Phone Bingo with a friend (or group of friends). Call a random person in your contacts and each player has to get the selected list of words below into the conversation, cross them off, then shout 'Phone Bingo!'

GIRAFFE

SHOELACE

CHICKEN WING

UNICYCLE

EAR WAX

USE YOUR OLD NAIL VARNISH TO PAINT THIS PAGE

POINTLESS PAGE!

WHEN YOU SEE THIS PAGE FILL IT IN WITH WHATEVER YOU WANT!

WRITE DOWN WHATEVER YOU DID ON THE PREVIOUS PAGE AND THE REASON WHY YOU DID IT

_____

_____

_____

_____

_____

_____

_____

_____

_____

_____

_____

_____

_____

_____

_____

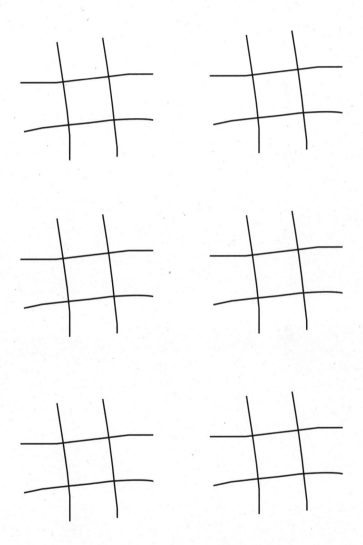

MUSIC MAKER!

WRITE A SELECTION OF LYRICS FROM YOUR TOP
FIVE FAVOURITE SONGS AND MAKE UP A NEW SONG:

HEAD, BODY AND TAILS

WITH A GROUP OF FRIENDS, TAKE IT IN TURN TO DRAW THE PARTS OF [PERSON] ON THE PAGE BELOW. BEGIN WITH THE HEAD, FOLD THE PAGE AND PASS TO W[HOE]VER IS ON YOUR RIGHT. ONCE YOU'VE COMPLETED THE HEAD, SHOULDERS, BODY, LEG[S AN]D FEET, OPEN IT UP TO REVEAL YOUR CREATION!

TEAR HERE

HEAD

[SHO]ULDERS

LEG[S]

FEET

ANAGRAM PAGE!

Un-scramble the following Pointless anagrams:

GOBLIN TOPLESS

_____

EARN DUVET

_____

MIMES MUTER

_____

HAT PAY SPY

_____

HAPPY HOG ROT

_____

WRITE A POEM...

BRAIN TEASERS...

TRY YOUR BEST TO SOLVE THESE:

WHAT TRAVELS AROUND THE WORLD BUT STAYS IN THE CORNER?

_____

WHAT GETS WETTER AND WETTER THE MORE IT DRIES? _____

WHAT CAN YOU CATCH BUT CAN'T THROW?

_____

WHICH WORD IN THE DICTIONARY IS SPELLED INCORRECTLY? _____

YOU CAN HOLD IT WITHOUT USING YOUR ARMS. WHAT IS IT?

_____

NOTES

USE THIS PAGE WHEN YOU NEED SOME PAPER!

POINTLESS PAGE!

WHEN YOU SEE THIS PAGE FILL IT IN WITH WHATEVER YOU WANT!

TURN TO PAGE 15

TURN TO PAGE 15

DESIGN YOUR OWN ALBUM COVER

MY JOURNAL THIS WEEK

WEEK STARTING ___ / / ___

WRITE DOWN ONE SENTENCE TO DESCRIBE EACH DAY THIS WEEK.

MONDAY _____

_____

TUESDAY _____

_____

WEDNESDAY _____

_____

THURSDAY _____

_____

FRIDAY _____

_____

SATURDAY _____

_____

SUNDAY _____

_____

CONSEQUENCES...

GAME 1:

(SEE RULES ON PAGE 40)

FOLD HERE

GAME 2:

FOLD HERE

TEAR THE CORNERS OFF THIS PAGE

404 PAGE NOT FOUND

HOLE-PUNCH THIS PAGE!

CREATE SOME ART USING A HOLE-PUNCH!

ROCK, PAPER, SCISSORS

KEEP SCORE HERE:

PLAYER 1	PLAYER 2

WINNER:

_____

DRAW AROUND YOUR OWN HAND...

THUMB WARS

KEEP SCORE HERE:

PLAYER 1	PLAYER 2

 WINNER: _____

PEOPLE WATCHING PAGE...

TICK WHEN YOU SEE:

☐ SOMEONE WEARING FLIP-FLOPS

☐ SOMEONE RIDING A SKATEBOARD

☐ TOO MUCH PDA (PUBLIC DISPLAY OF AFFECTION)

☐ SOMEONE WEARING A BANDANA

☐ SOMEONE RUNNING FOR A BUS

☐ A TREE TALLER THAN YOUR HOUSE

TURN THIS PAGE WITH YOUR NOSE

TURN TO PAGE 190

DOODLE

FILL THIS PAGE WITH DOODLES

HEAD TENNIS

LOOK RIGHT!

$\longrightarrow$

LOOK LEFT!

DRAW YOUR WEEK IN A STORYBOARD

DRAW HERE

WRITE HERE

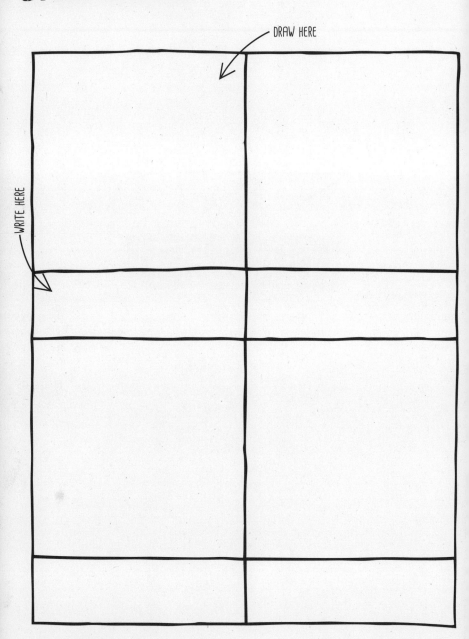

F-TEST!

COUNT EVERY "F" IN THE FOLLOWING TEXT

FUNNY FRIENDS ARE
THE RESULT OF YEARS
OF SCIENTIFIC STUDY
COMBINED WITH THE
EXPERIENCE OF YEARS...

WRITE WHAT YOU DID TODAY

...WITH YOUR OPPOSITE WRITING HAND

WHAT'S THE FIRST THING YOU DO IN THE MORNING AND WHY?

WHEN YOU SEE THIS PAGE FILL IT IN WITH WHATEVER YOU WANT!

RANDOM TWEET!

WHENEVER YOU OPEN
THE BOOK OR PASS
THIS PAGE YOU HAVE TO
TWEET SOMETHING WITH

#THEPOINTLESSBOOK

DRAW A 'SELFIE'

TIME CAPSULE

PUT SOMETHING BETWEEN THESE TWO PAGES
AND GLUE THEM TOGETHER. WRITE A DATE ON
THE NEXT PAGE AND DO NOT OPEN UNTIL THEN.

DO NOT OPEN THIS CAPSULE UNTIL

DRAW YOUR PET

(IF YOU DON'T HAVE A PET DRAW A GOLDFISH!)

WITH A FRIEND SEE HOW LONG YOU CAN DIP A BISCUIT IN YOUR CUP OF TEA BEFORE IT BREAKS OFF

KEEP SCORE HERE:

YOU	FRIEND

WRITE DOWN SOME FUNNY OVERHEARD CONVERSATIONS...

DRAW A LANDMARK...

...FROM A PLACE YOU WOULD LIKE TO VISIT

CRAZY COCKTAIL

MAKE THE WEIRDEST COCKTAIL POSSIBLE! JOT DOWN WHAT YOU'VE PUT IN IT (KETCHUP, MUSTARD...) AND RATE HOW IT TASTED OUT OF 10.

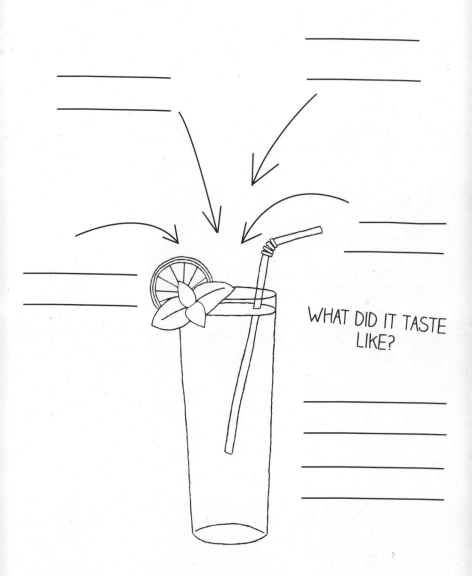

WHAT DID IT TASTE LIKE?

MAKE A FACE USING MAGAZINE CUT-OUTS...

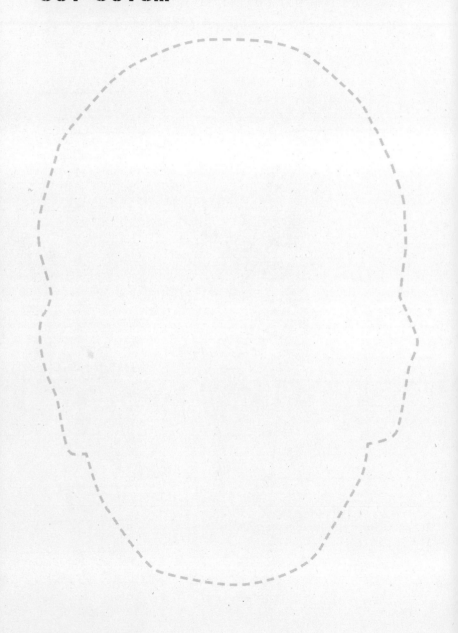

MAKE A SMOOTHIE FROM WHATEVER YOU HAVE IN THE FRIDGE...

INGREDIENTS:

_____
_____
_____
_____
_____
_____
_____
_____
_____

WHAT DID IT TASTE LIKE?

_____
_____
_____
_____
_____
_____

LIST YOUR TOP FIVE FILMS

1.

2.

3.

4.

5.

MY FIRST...

1. WORD MUMMA

2. FRIEND ASHTON

3. PET brain   jish

4. KISS MOM

5. FEAR A.G

6. JOB 1

7. PHONE NOKIA

STICK A PHOTO HERE OF WHEN
YOU WERE YOUNG

DRAW WHAT YOU'D LIKE TO BE WHEN YOU'RE OLDER

On the board below write down the name of four people (two you like, two you dislike), four countries, and four random numbers. Grab a pen and tap inside the box until a nominated player says 'stop!' Count the dots and, beginning with 'M', use this number to cross off the answers surrounding the box, crossing off an answer every time you get to your number. The game is complete when one answer remains in each panel...

MASH

MANSION APARTMENT SHED HOUSE

NAMES

COUNTRIES

KIDS

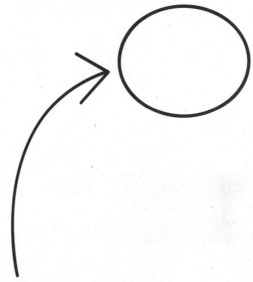

STICK CHEWING GUM
HERE AND FOLD THE CORNER

WHAT DID I DO ON THIS DAY...?

NEW YEAR'S DAY _PARTY_

EASTER MONDAY _CHILL_

ST PATRICK'S DAY _/_

MIDSUMMER'S DAY _/_

AUGUST BANK HOLIDAY _/_

WHO WOULD YOU INVITE TO YOUR DREAM DINNER PARTY?

...CHOOSE ANYONE YOU LIKE, DEAD OR ALIVE.

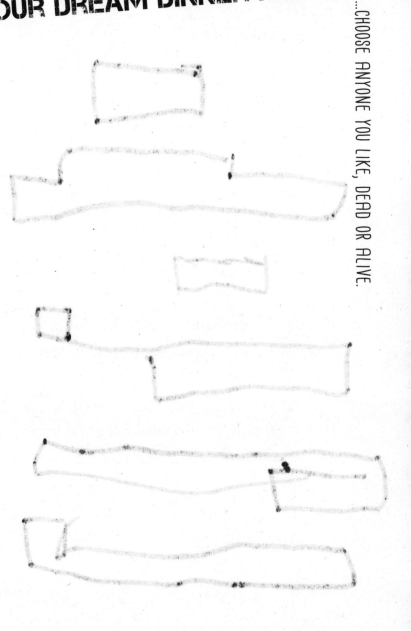

WOULD YOU RATHER...

1) Be boiling hot or freezing cold?

2) Have your computer memory wiped or have your past and future web browsing history available to everyone?

3) Drink a cup of public swimming pool water or sea water?

4) Hiccup for the rest of your life or feel like you have to sneeze but can't for the rest of your life?

5) Listen to one song for the rest of your life or never listen to the same song twice?

6) Not be able to use the internet or not be able to listen to music?

SNOG, MARRY, AVOID...

SNOG ☐

MARRY ☐

AVOID ☐

SNOG ☐

MARRY ☐

AVOID ☐

SNOG ☐

MARRY ☐

AVOID ☐

DESCRIBE YOURSELF IN FIVE WORDS...

EPIC

FAST

'FISHERMAN

HOT

SIX PACA

USE THIS PAGE
WHEN YOU
DESPERATELY NEED
TOILET ~~PAPER~~

...DON'T FORGET TO FLUSH...

TURN THIS PAGE WITH YOUR TOE

WHEN YOU SEE THIS PAGE FILL IT IN WITH WHATEVER YOU WANT!

POINTLESS PAGE!

SEE ALFIE'S JOKE

PB1

DID THEY:

1. LAUGH
2. CRY
3. VOMIT
4. RUN AWAY

ANAGRAM ANSWERS

GOBLIN TOPLESS

POINTLESS BLOG

EARN DUVET

ADVENTURE

MIMES MUTER

SUMMER TIME

HAT PAY SPY

STAY HAPPY

HAPPY HOG ROT

PHOTOGRAPHY

BRAIN-TEASER ANSWERS

WHAT TRAVELS AROUND THE WORLD BUT STAYS IN THE CORNER?

A POSTAGE STAMP

WHAT GETS WETTER AND WETTER THE MORE IT DRIES?

A TOWEL

WHAT CAN YOU CATCH BUT CAN'T THROW?

A COLD

WHICH WORD IN THE DICTIONARY IS SPELLED INCORRECTLY?

INCORRECTLY

YOU CAN HOLD IT WITHOUT USING YOUR ARMS. WHAT IS IT?

YOUR BREATH

WRITE FIVE THINGS YOU LIKE BEST ABOUT YOURSELF AND WHY...

1. _____
_____
_____
_____

2. _____
_____
_____
_____

3. _____
_____
_____
_____

4. _____
_____
_____
_____

5. _____
_____
_____
_____

SPARE PAPER...

...USE THIS PAGE WHEN
YOU NEED SOME PAPER

CREATE SOME ART HERE WITH THE HOLES FROM THE HOLE-PUNCH PAGE!

(FROM PAGE 123)

BASKETBALL CHALLENGE

CRUMPLE UP THIS PAGE AND THROW PAPER IN A BASKET-BIN

TOP FIVE THINGS...

...THAT MAKE YOU WANT TO VOMIT.

1. _____

2. _____

3. _____

4. _____

5. _____

CUT OUT NEWSPAPER HEADLINES...

...AND MAKE A STORY HERE!

WRITE A COMPLIMENT...

...RIP OUT THIS PAGE AND GIVE IT TO A STRANGER.

FILL THIS PAGE

WITH THINGS YOU LOVE...

SPOT THE DIFFERENCE ANSWERS...

WORD SEARCH ANSWERS...

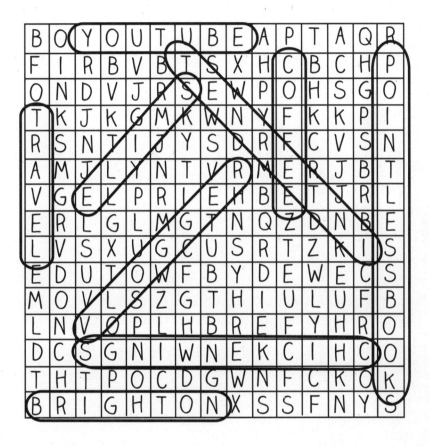

B	O	Y	O	U	T	U	B	E	A	P	T	A	Q	R
F	I	R	B	V	B	T	S	X	H	C	B	C	H	P
O	N	D	V	J	R	S	E	W	P	O	H	S	G	O
T	K	J	K	G	M	K	W	N	Y	F	K	K	P	I
R	S	N	T	I	J	Y	S	D	R	F	C	V	S	N
A	M	J	L	Y	N	T	V	R	M	E	R	J	B	T
V	G	E	L	P	R	I	E	H	B	E	T	J	R	L
E	R	L	G	L	M	G	T	N	Q	Z	D	N	B	E
L	V	S	X	U	G	C	U	S	R	T	Z	K	I	S
E	D	U	T	O	W	F	B	Y	D	E	W	E	C	S
M	O	V	L	S	Z	G	T	H	I	U	L	U	F	B
L	N	V	O	P	L	H	B	R	E	F	Y	H	R	O
D	C	S	G	N	I	W	N	E	K	C	I	H	C	O
T	H	T	P	O	C	D	G	W	N	F	C	K	O	K
B	R	I	G	H	T	O	N	X	S	S	F	N	Y	S

YOUTUBE   SMILE   COFFEE

VLOGGER   BRIGHTON   INTERNET

POINTLESS BOOK   TRAVEL   CHICKEN WINGS

BALANCE THE BOOK ON YOUR HEAD CHALLENGE!

INSTRUCTIONS:

1. CLOSE YOUR POINTLESS BOOK (NOT NOW - WAIT UNTIL YOU'VE READ ALL OF THE INSTRUCTIONS FIRST!).

2. STAND IN AN OPEN SPACE AND MAKE SURE THERE AREN'T ANY OBSTACLES IN YOUR WAY.

3. PLACE THE BOOK ON THE MIDDLE OF YOUR HEAD AND TAKE A STEP FORWARD.

HOW MANY STEPS CAN YOU TAKE?

TWEET YOUR BEST TIME TO #THEPOINTLESSBOOK

TURN TO PAGE 34

TURN TO PAGE 34

DRAW THE HYBRID ANIMALS

DRAW THESE HYBRID ANIMALS: A ZEDONKEY, A GORILLAROO, A CABBIT AND A FROGODILE!

A GEEP

CELEBRITY FISH NAME GAME

FILL THESE PAGES WITH AS MANY CELEBRITY FISH NAMES YOU AND YOUR FRIENDS CAN THINK OF! HERE ARE A FEW TO START YOU OFF:

TUNA TURNER

MUSSEL CROWE

CALAMARI DIAZ

GIVE THIS BOOK TO A FRIEND...

...AND ASK THEM TO DESCRIBE YOU IN THREE WORDS:

DOODLE TIME!

TURN TO PAGE 130

SUGGEST MORE WAYS THIS BOOK CAN BE POINTLESS...

1.

2.

3.

4.

5.

6.

THE Pointless Book 2

CONTINUED BY ALFIE DEYES
FINISHED BY YOU

BLINK
bringing you closer

THE POINTLESS BOOK 2 APP

WATCH ALFIE IN ACTION

PB2

SCAN ME

THIS BOOK
BELONGS TO:

GUCA

DRAW YOUR FAVOURITE FOOD...

HAVE YOU EVER...

SEE ALFIE'S CHOICES — PB2

	Y	N
BEEN ON A ROAD TRIP?	☒	☐
WEED IN THE SEA?	☒	☐
PRETENDED TO BE A MANNEQUIN IN A SHOP?	☐	☒
CHEATED WHILST PLAYING A GAME?	☒	☐
FALLEN ASLEEP ON PUBLIC TRANSPORT?	☐	☒
GONE WITHOUT SHOWERING FOR OVER A WEEK?	☒	☐
STAYED AWAKE ALL NIGHT?	☐	☒
EATEN FOOD THAT HAS FALLEN ON THE FLOOR?	☒	☐
SPIED ON YOUR NEIGHBOURS?	☒	☐
MADE A PRANK PHONE CALL?	☒	☐
SENT SOMEONE THE WRONG TEXT?	☐	☒
HAD A BAD HAIRCUT?	☒	☐

DRAW YOUR DREAM TREEHOUSE...

£ WHAT WOULD YOU £ DO IF YOU WON A MILLION POUNDS?

THE BLINDFOLD MAKE-UP CHALLENGE

WATCH ALFIE'S MAKE-UP CHALLENGE
PB²

THIS IS ONE OF THE GREATEST CHALLENGES EVER! FIND A FRIEND AND ASK THEM TO PUT A BLINDFOLD ON YOU. GRAB SOME MAKE-UP AND DECORATE THEIR FACE. BE AS CREATIVE AS YOU LIKE!

TWEET YOUR ATTEMPTS TO #POINTLESSMAKEUP

WARNING LABEL!

IF YOU HAD A WARNING LABEL WHAT WOULD IT BE?
(FOR EXAMPLE: DON'T WAKE ME UP BEFORE 10AM!)

WARNING!

17 # TODAY'S Punch

DATE: #3 April 2016

FIRST THOUGHT: Wow Im tired!.

BREAKFAST: BACON, EGGS, TOAST

BEST MOMENT: ~~EATING~~ FOOTBALL

FAVOURITE TV SHOW: Vampire Diaries

TREAT: Chocolate crossant

BOOK: DEAMON RAOD

CHALLENGE: LIVING IN THE WILD

PAIR OF SHOES: ALL STARS

GOSSIP: I burnt my finger

BEST CONVERSATION: Realizing my HW
was all DONE.

JOKE: ___

ACHIEVEMENT: Showering before 9

BEST TEXT: ___

GOOD DEED: I Played football
with guees.

THE POINTLESS PHONE CHALLENGE

IT'S TIME FOR THE POINTLESS PHONE CHALLENGE! THIS GAME IS A LOT OF FUN AND CAN BE ABSOLUTELY HILARIOUS! HERE'S HOW TO PLAY:

1. IN THE BOXES BELOW, WRITE SIX OF THE MOST OUTRAGEOUS THINGS YOU'VE EVER HEARD.

2. GRAB YOUR MOBILE PHONE AND OPEN YOUR CONTACTS.

3. FIND A FRIEND AND ASK THEM TO DO THE SAME WITH THEIR MOBILE PHONE.

4. TAKE IT IN TURNS TO SCROLL THROUGH YOUR CONTACTS LIST WITHOUT LOOKING. WHEN THE OTHER PLAYER SAYS 'STOP', YOU HAVE TO CALL OR TEXT YOUR CONTACT, SAYING/WRITING ONE OF THE LINES BELOW...

INVENT A CATCHPHRASE

EVERYONE HAS A CATCHPHRASE THESE DAYS. TRY TO THINK OF ONE BASED ON YOUR NAME OR YOUR FRIEND'S NAME. IT'S EASIER THAN YOU THINK!

OH MY DEYES!

_____

_____

_____

_____

_____

_____

_____

_____

_____

POINTLESS RIDDLES

HERE ARE A COUPLE OF BRAIN TEASERS FOR YOU TO SOLVE. WRITE THE ANSWERS IN THE SPACE PROVIDED:

1. I TRAVEL A LOT – IN FACT I'VE BEEN TO EVERY COUNTRY IN THE WORLD! I'M INVISIBLE BUT YOU CAN SOMETIMES SEE ME.

   AIR

2. HOW MANY SECONDS ARE IN ONE YEAR?

   $60 \times 60 \times 24 \times 365 =$

3. WHAT GOES UP WHEN THE RAIN COMES DOWN?

   WORMS

4. I'M AN ANCIENT INVENTION THAT ALLOWS YOU TO SEE THROUGH WALLS. WHAT AM I?

   WINDOW

MAKE UP A STORY USING THESE WORDS...

(AND A FEW OF YOUR OWN!)

WORLD, PIZZA, FINGERNAIL, COMB, SLEEP, HILARIOUS, HAIR, TWEET, FRIENDS, FRECKLE

SCAN HERE

PB2

COMPLETE THE MAZE!

START

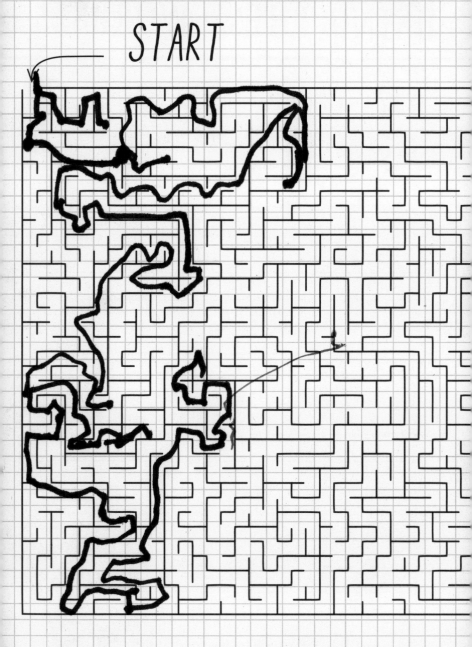

GRAB A PENCIL AND TRACE YOUR ROUTE THROUGH THE POINTLESS MAZE. BEGIN AT THE START POINT AND MAKE YOUR WAY THROUGH TO THE END WITHOUT LIFTING YOUR PENCIL OFF THE PAGE!

END ⟶

CURRENTLY I'M

READING: THIS BOOK

WATCHING: NOTHING

SINGING: 7x0ars

THINKING: a Footie

EATING: NOTHING

WISHING:

WANTING:

NEEDING:

TEXTING:

DRINKING:

TWEETING:

WRITING: IN THIS BOOK

LEARNING: STUFF ATSCHOOL

HOPING: STUFF

CALLING: NO ONE

DON'T BREAK THE CHAIN

WATCH ALFIE IN ACTION
PB2

LET'S PLAY A GAME OF WORD ASSOCIATION. MATCH THE WORD TO THE PREVIOUS ONE WITHOUT STOPPING. HOW MANY WORDS CAN YOU DO IN ONE MINUTE?

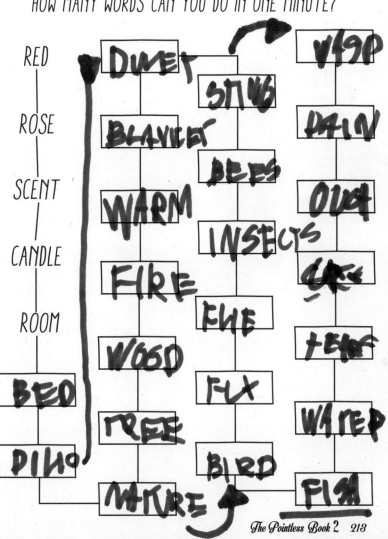

RED — ROSE — SCENT — CANDLE — ROOM

BED

PILLO

DUVET · SNUG · WASP

BLANKET · BEES · PAIN

WARM · INSECTS · OUCH

FIRE · FLIE · LIFE

WOOD · FLY · TEARS

TREE · BIRD · WATER

NATURE · FISH

DRAW YOUR DREAM HOUSE

FIVE CITIES I'D LIKE TO VISIT...

SCAN HERE
TO SEE
ALFIE'S
TOP 5

PB2

1 _____

2 _____

3 _____

4 _____

5 _____

MY FANTASY DAY

8AM: _____

10AM: _____

12PM: _____

2PM: _____

4PM: _____

6PM: _____

8PM: _____

10PM: _____

MUFFIN IN A MUG

INGREDIENTS:

1 CUP OF FLOUR
1 TBSP BROWN SUGAR
1/2 TSP BAKING POWDER
1/8 TSP SALT
A PINCH OF CINNAMON
1/2 TBSP BUTTER
2 TBSP MILK
1-2 TBSP FROZEN BLUEBERRIES

1. CHOOSE A MUG. ADD THE FLOUR, BROWN SUGAR, BAKING POWDER, SALT, AND CINNAMON AND GIVE IT A GOOD MIX.

2. ADD THE BUTTER AND USE YOUR FINGERS TO SQUISH IT ALL TOGETHER UNTIL ALL OF THOSE BUTTER CHUNKS HAVE DISAPPEARED.

3. ADD THE MILK INTO THE BUTTERY-FLOURY MIXTURE AND STIR UNTIL IT'S SMOOTH AND MOIST (DON'T WORRY IF IT LOOKS A BIT DRY, JUST ADD MORE MILK!). SCATTER THE BLUEBERRIES ON TOP AND PUSH THEM DOWN INTO THE MIXTURE.

4. PLACE YOUR MUG OF DELICIOUSNESS IN THE MICROWAVE AND COOK ON THE HIGHEST SETTING FOR TWO MINUTES.

5. ONCE YOU HEAR THE 'DING' IT'S READY TO EAT!

POINTLESS OPPOSITES

EVERYTHING HAS AN OPPOSITE - YOU JUST NEED TO USE YOUR IMAGINATION. WHAT'S THE OPPOSITE OF A CUP? A SAUCER! WHAT'S THE OPPOSITE OF A DOG? A CAT! EVEN PEOPLE HAVE AN OPPOSITE - YOU JUST NEED TO BE CREATIVE. HERE ARE A FEW TO GET YOU STARTED:

AL-FIE DEYES   EARLY BIRD-FREE NIGHTS

TINIE TEMPAH   LARGE HAPPINESS

TAYLOR SWIFT   _____

PROFESSOR GREEN   _____

JAMIE OLIVER   _____

_____   _____

_____   _____

_____   _____

_____

DRAW A PICTURE...

...ONLY USING TRIANGLES

SCAN HERE
TO SEE
ALFIE'S
PICTURE

PB2

DRAW YOURSELF IN 50 YEARS...

POINTLESS PHOTOBOMB!

GRAB YOUR POINTLESS BOOK 2 AND TRY TO SNEAK INTO SOMEONE'S PICTURE. GOT ANY GREAT PHOTOBOMBS? TWEET THEM TO

#POINTLESSPHOTO

MAKE UP A POINTLESS SONG

EVERYONE HAS A SONG INSIDE THEM! GET CREATIVE AND PEN A POINTLESS TUNE. YOU CAN BASE IT ON A POPULAR SONG OR EVEN MAKE ONE UP FROM SCRATCH!

LEARN TO TALK SDRAWKCAB!

GNIKLAT SDRAWKCAB SI
ENO FO S'EFIL TSETAERG
STFIG. TSUJ ETARAPES EHT
SDROW OTNI SELBALLYS
DNA YAS TI KCIUQ! DNA
REBMEMER STNANOSNOC TA
EHT GNINNIGEB FO SDROW
ERA TNELIS!

MOONWALKING LESSON!

THERE'S A TIME AND A PLACE FOR A MOONWALK: WHEN YOU'RE ON THE DANCEFLOOR; WHEN YOU'RE WALKING TO THE SHOPS; WHEN YOU'RE LEAVING CLASS AFTER ACING AN EXAM. BUT NOT EVERYONE KNOWS HOW TO DO IT PROPERLY. HERE'S A LESSON ON LIFE'S GREATEST DANCE MOVE...

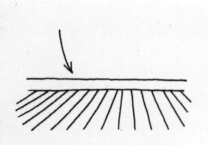

1. FIND A NICE OPEN SPACE (PREFERABLY A HARD WOODEN FLOOR).

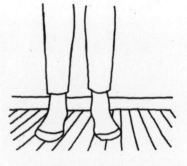

2. STAND AT ONE END OF THE ROOM WITH YOUR FEET SHOULDER-WIDTH APART.

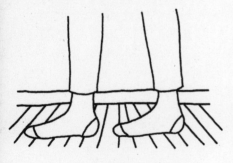

3. PLACE ONE FOOT IN FRONT OF THE OTHER.

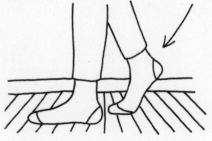

4. LIFT THE HEEL OF YOUR BACK FOOT OFF THE FLOOR.

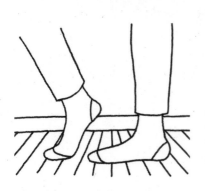

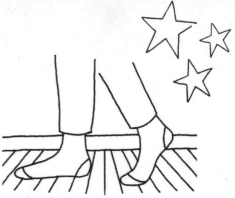

5. SLIDE YOUR FRONT FOOT ALONGSIDE YOUR BACK FOOT UNTIL IT'S BEHIND YOU.

6. ONCE YOUR SLIDING FOOT IS BEHIND YOU, SHIFT POSITION SO THE HEEL OF YOUR SLIDING FOOT IS OFF THE FLOOR AND THE HEEL OF YOUR STANDING FOOT IS FLAT.

7. REPEAT.

8. PUT ON 'BILLIE JEAN' AND SHOW YOUR FRIENDS.

VIDEO-MIME CHALLENGE

TWEET A VIDEO OF YOURSELF
MIMING ALONG TO YOUR
FAVOURITE SONG TO

#POINTLESSMIME

FACE IMPRESSIONS

THERE ARE IMPRESSIONS AND THEN THERE ARE FACE IMPRESSIONS. USING ONE FACIAL EXPRESSION, DO AN IMPRESSION OF THE FOLLOWING ANIMALS...

HAPPY DOG

CONFUSED HORSE

SAD CAT

WORRIED PENGUIN

MAKE UP SOME MORE OF YOUR OWN!

ALFIE'S JUICE RECIPE

INGREDIENTS:

1 CUP OF BLACKBERRIES.
1 CUP OF BLUEBERRIES.
1 CUP OF RASPBERRIES.
1 TEASPOON OF HONEY.
1 CUP OF WATER.
SOME ICE CUBES!

METHOD:

1. FIRST, ADD ALL THE INGREDIENTS TO THE BLENDER AND BLEND UNTIL SMOOTH.

2. GRAB A GLASS, HOLD A STRAINER OVER IT AND POUR THE JUICE THROUGH IT.

3. POP A FEW LEFTOVER BERRIES ON TOP AND YOU'RE DONE!

NAMES IN A HAT

GRAB SOME FRIENDS (AND A COUPLE OF HATS!) FOR A GAME OF CHARADES – WITH A DIFFERENCE. HERE'S HOW YOU PLAY:

1. CUT OUT THE TABS BELOW AND DISTRIBUTE THREE TO EVERY PLAYER.

2. EACH FRIEND THEN WRITES THE NAME OF THREE FAMOUS PEOPLE OR CHARACTERS AND PLACES THE NAMES IN HAT ONE.

3. SPLIT THE GROUP INTO TWO TEAMS AND ONCE YOU'RE READY, NOMINATE ONE PERSON TO GO FIRST.

4. IN ROUND ONE THE PLAYER HAS 30 SECONDS TO DESCRIBE THE NAME USING CHARADES – NO TALKING, ONLY ACTING! WHEN HIS OR HER TEAM GUESSES THE CORRECT NAME, THE PLAYER PLACES THE CORRECT TAB INTO HAT TWO.

5. AFTER 30 SECONDS IT'S THE OTHER TEAM'S GO. MAKE SURE THAT THE FIRST TEAM KEEPS A TALLY OF HOW MANY NAMES THEY GUESSED.

6. ONCE ALL THE NAMES HAVE BEEN PICKED FROM HAT ONE IT'S TIME FOR ROUND TWO. IN THIS ROUND THE PLAYER HAS 30 SECONDS TO DESCRIBE THE FAMOUS PERSON OR CHARACTER WITHOUT SAYING THE NAME ON THE TAB.

7. AS WITH THE PREVIOUS ROUND, ONCE THE TEAM GUESSES THE CORRECT TAB, THE PLAYER PLACES THE PIECE OF PAPER BACK INTO HAT ONE. AND REMEMBER TO KEEP A POINTS TALLY!

8. ONCE ALL THE NAMES HAVE BEEN PICKED IT IS TIME FOR ROUND THREE. THIS TIME EACH PLAYER HAS TO DESCRIBE THE NAME OF THE FAMOUS PERSON OR CELEBRITY USING ONE WORD.

9. REPEAT THE PROCESS JUST LIKE THE PREVIOUS ROUNDS.

10. THE WINNING GROUP IS THE TEAM WITH THE MOST POINTS AT THE END OF THE GAME!

20 FACTS ABOUT ME

SCAN HERE FOR ALFIE'S 20 FACTS

PB2

1. _____

2. _____

3. _____

4. _____

5. _____

6. _____

7. _____

8. _____

9. _____

10. _____

11. _____

12. _____

13. _____

14. _____

15. _____

16. _____

17. _____

18. _____

19. _____

20. _____

OPTICAL ILLUSIONS

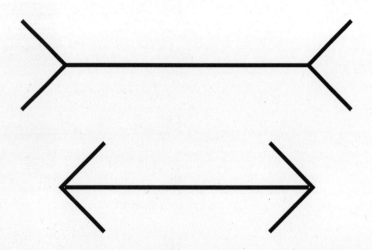

THE TOP LINE APPEARS LONGER THAN THE BOTTOM
ONE BUT IS ACTUALLY THE SAME LENGTH.

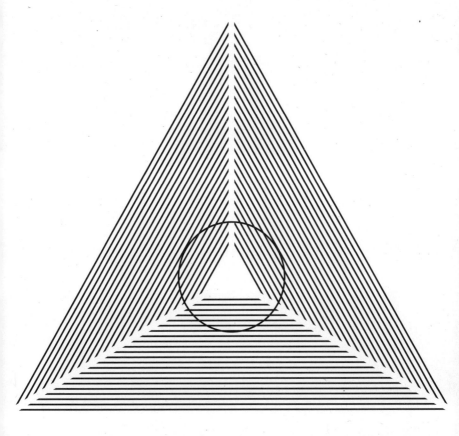

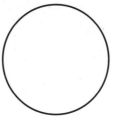

THE ROUND CIRCLE ON THE LINES IN THE TRIANGLE IS
IDENTICAL TO THE ONE BELOW.

PAPER PIZZA TOPPINGS

MMMM PIZZA. MAKE YOUR OWN USING THE CUT OUT
TOPPINGS AND BASE BELOW. YOU CAN MAKE UP A NAME
FOR YOUR CREATION TOO!

NAME:

DRAW A HORSE...

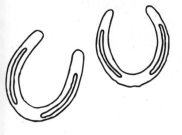

SCAN HERE
TO SEE
ALFIE'S
HORSE

PB2

HOW WELL DO YOU KNOW YOUR BEST FRIEND?

WRITE DOWN THE ANSWERS TO THE QUESTIONS BELOW AND
HAND THEM TO YOUR FRIEND TO MARK...

1. WRITE DOWN THEIR PHONE NUMBER, BY HEART!

2. WHAT IS THE NAME OF THEIR FIRST CRUSH?

3. WHAT IS THEIR FAVOURITE FOOD?

4. WHAT IS THEIR MIDDLE NAME?

5. WHAT IS THEIR FAVOURITE FILM?

6. LIST THREE THINGS THEY WOULD NEVER LEAVE HOME WITHOUT?

7. WHAT IS THEIR BIGGEST PET HATE?

8. WHAT IS THEIR DREAM JOB?

9. WHERE WOULD THEY MOST LIKE TO LIVE?

10. WHAT IS THEIR MOST EMBARRASSING MOMENT?

11. WHAT TOPPINGS WOULD THEY WANT ON THEIR PIZZA?

12. WHO IS THEIR FAVOURITE YOUTUBER?

TRY NOT TO LAUGH CHALLENGE

FIND A FRIEND WHO YOU FIND PARTICULARLY FUNNY, SIT FACING EACH OTHER AND SEE HOW LONG IT TAKES BEFORE THEY CAN MAKE YOU LAUGH. RECORD YOUR PERSONAL BESTS BELOW...

PERSONAL BEST 1: _____

PERSONAL BEST 2: _____

PERSONAL BEST 3: _____

PERSONAL BEST 4: _____

PERSONAL BEST 5: _____

PERSONAL BEST 6: _____

WRITE YOUR OWN RECIPE

NAME: _____

INGREDIENTS:

_____
_____
_____
_____
_____
_____
_____
_____
_____

METHOD:

_____
_____
_____
_____
_____
_____
_____
_____
_____
_____
_____
_____
_____
_____
_____
_____
_____
_____
_____
_____

WHAT DID IT TASTE LIKE?

_____
_____
_____

SECRET PAGE...

...FIND THE KEY TO UNLOCK THE BOX

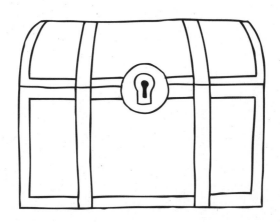

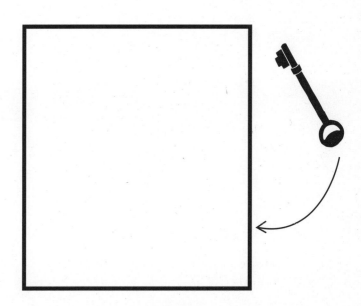

DRAW
SOMETHING THAT
REMINDS YOU OF...

YOUR BEST
FRIEND...

ALFIE DEYES...

YOUR MUM...

YOUR FAVOURITE
SONG...

YOUR FAVOURITE
MEMORY...

YOUR HOMETOWN...

HANG MAN

IT'S TIME FOR A CLASSIC GAME OF HANG MAN...

C A B

E I O d G P S N B

7 WAYS TO IMPROVE YOUR LIFE...

SCAN HERE TO SEE ALFIE'S CHOICES

PB2

1. _____
_____

2. _____
_____

3. _____
_____

4. _____
_____

5. _____
_____

6. _____
_____

7. _____
_____

10 THINGS TO DO THIS SUMMER...

1. _____

2. _____

3. _____

4. _____

5. _____

6. _____

7. _____

8. _____

9. _____

10. _____

5 THINGS YOU WOULD CHANGE ABOUT THE WORLD

1. _____
_____
_____

2. _____
_____
_____

3. _____
_____
_____

4. _____
_____
_____

5. _____
_____
_____

THE BLINDFOLD DRAWING CHALLENGE

A MEERKAT

WITH A FRIEND DRAW THE FOLLOWING BLINDFOLDED...

SCAN HERE TO SEE ALFIE'S ATTEMPT

PB2

A FRIEND

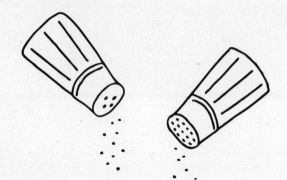

SEASON THIS PAGE...

...WITH SALT AND PEPPER

SPECIAL WEEKEND DIARY

FRIDAY _____
_____
_____
_____
_____
_____
_____

SATURDAY _____
_____
_____
_____
_____
_____
_____

SUNDAY _____
_____
_____
_____
_____
_____
_____

A DAY IN THE LIFE OF YOU...

DATE: _____

_____

_____

_____

_____

_____

_____

_____

_____

_____

_____

_____

_____

_____

_____

_____

_____

_____

_____

_____

THE NUMBERS GAME

SPELL OUT THE NUMBERS – HOW FAR CAN YOU GET BEFORE YOU REACH THE LETTER 'A'?

ONE
TWO
THREE

L F R J M A
O E D Z G Q
P

SHADOW PUPPETS

HAVE YOU EVER TRIED MAKING A SHADOW PUPPET ON THE WALL? ALL YOU NEED IS A TORCH, A DARK ROOM AND A CLEAR SPACE UPON WHICH TO PERFORM YOUR AMAZING PUPPETRY! HERE ARE A FEW CREATURES TO GET YOU STARTED...

A CHICKEN

A SWAN

A BULL

A PARROT

A BUTTERFLY

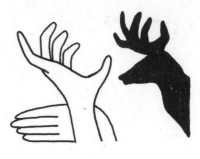

A STAG

A DOG

A HORSE

A RABBIT

A SNAIL

IF YOU WERE THE OTHER SEX WHAT WOULD YOUR NAME BE?

MALE

Gianluca

FEMALE

Petra

DESIGN YOUR OWN TRAINER

SCAN HERE TO SEE YOUR DESIGN

PB2

BRING OUT YOUR INNER-DESIGNER BY COLOURING IN THIS TRAINER.

MAKE SURE YOU COLOUR WITHIN THE LINES!

CHATTERBOX CHALLENGE

CHECK OUT THE CHATTERBOX CHALLENGE! USING THE
INSTRUCTIONS BELOW AND ON THE PAGE OPPOSITE, CONSTRUCT
YOUR OWN CHATTERBOX. DON'T FORGET TO ADD A FEW DARES
TO YOUR CHATTERBOX TO MAKE IT EVEN MORE FUN!

1.
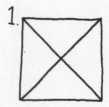

FOLD THE OPPOSITE
CORNERS TOGETHER.
UNFOLD SO YOU HAVE A
SQUARE WITH A X CREASE.

2.
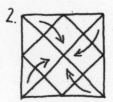

FOLD CORNERS INTO THE
CENTRE SO POINTS MEET.
TURNOVER AND FOLD TO
THE CENTRE AGAIN.

3.
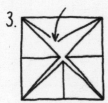

TURN YOUR SQUARE OVER
AND FOLD EACH OF THE FOUR
CORNERS TO THE CENTRE
POINT AGAIN SO THAT YOUR
SQUARE NOW STARTS TO LOOK
LIKE THE DIAGRAM ABOVE.

4.
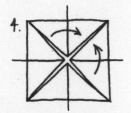

NOW FOLD IN HALF,
UNFOLD AND FOLD
AGAIN.

5.
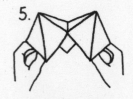

PUT YOUR FINGER AND
THUMB UNDER THE FLAPS
AND PUSH TOGETHER TO
MAKE YOUR CHATTERBOX.

CUT OUT THE SQUARE ON THE DOTTED LINES!

ADD COLOUR HERE

ADD YOUR DARES HERE

FAVOURITE
WORDS

LIST YOUR FAVOURITE WORDS HERE:

POINTLESS PATH PUZZLE

HELP NALA FIND HER WAY TO HER TASTY TREAT!

HOW MANY CLOTHES CAN YOU PUT ON IN ONE GO?

LIST WHAT YOU'RE WEARING HERE:

ONCE YOU'VE COMPLETED THE CHALLENGE TWEET A PICTURE TO

#CLOTHESCHALLENGE

THE 'DO MORE OF WHAT MAKES YOU HAPPY' TRANSLATION PAGE!

THIS PAGE IS DEDICATED TO ALL OF ALFIE'S FOLLOWERS AROUND THE WORLD! HERE'S HIS FAVOURITE PHRASE – DO MORE OF WHAT MAKES YOU HAPPY! – IN TEN DIFFERENT LANGUAGES. NAME THE LANGUAGE!

多做什么使你快乐!

_____

MACHEN SIE MEHR VON DEM, WAS DICH GLÜCKLICH MACHT!

_____

FARE DI PIÙ DI QUELLO CHE TI RENDE FELICE!

_____

Κάντε περισσότερα από ό, τι σε κάνει ευτυχισμένο!

_____

FAIRE PLUS DE CE QUI VOUS REND HEUREUX!

_____

HACER MÁS DE LO QUE TE HACE FELIZ!

_____

IF YOU COULD SPEAK ANOTHER LANGUAGE WHAT WOULD IT BE?

_____

WHAT'S YOUR POPSTAR NAME?

COUNTRIES A - Z

IN THE LIST BELOW, NAME A COUNTRY BEGINNING WITH
EVERY LETTER OF THE ALPHABET...

A Argentina   M   Y

B Bermuda   N   Z

C Canada   O

D   P

E   Q

F   R

G   S

H   T

I   U

J   V

K   W

L   X

WHAT'S YOUR SUPERHERO POWER?

SCAN TO SEE ALFIE'S CHOICE

PB2

SPIDERMAN CAN CLIMB WALLS. SUPERMAN CAN FLY. WHAT WOULD YOURS BE?

IF YOU WERE AN ANIMAL...

DRAW WHAT YOU WOULD BE:

APPLE BOBBING

SCAN HERE TO SEE ALFIE'S ATTEMPTS PB2

LET'S HAVE A GAME OF APPLE BOBBING! HERE'S HOW TO PLAY:

1. GRAB SIX APPLES.

2. GRAB A BIG BOWL OF WATER.

3. MARK EACH APPLE WITH THE NUMBERS '1' TO '6'.

4. PLACE THE APPLES IN THE BOWL.

5. FIND A FRIEND.

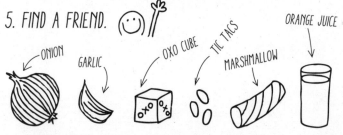

ONION   GARLIC   OXO CUBE   TIC TACS   MARSHMALLOW   ORANGE JUICE

6. FIND THREE THINGS YOU DON'T LIKE TO EAT – SUCH AS AN OXO CUBE, AN ONION AND A CLOVE OF GARLIC, AND THREE THINGS YOU LOVE TO EAT – SUCH AS A MARSHMALLOW, SOME TIC TACS AND A GLASS OF ORANGE JUICE. LABEL EACH ITEM NUMBERS '1' TO '6'.

7. TAKE IT IN TURNS TO FISH OUT THE APPLES WITHOUT USING YOUR HANDS. YOU THEN HAVE TO EAT OR DRINK THE ITEM THAT CORRESPONDS TO THE APPLE!

SNAKES AND LADDERS

THE AIM OF THE GAME IS TO BE THE FIRST PLAYER TO REACH SQUARE 90!

RULES OF PLAY:

1. EACH PLAYER ROLLS THE DICE. WHOEVER ROLLS THE HIGHEST NUMBER GETS TO PLAY FIRST.

2. PLAYER ONE, ROLL THE DICE AND MOVE FORWARD THAT NUMBER OF SPACES. IF YOU ROLL A 6 THEN YOU GET TO HAVE AN EXTRA TURN!

3. IF YOU LAND ON THE BASE OF A LADDER THEN YOU CAN CLIMB RIGHT UP TO THE TOP OF IT (HOORAY!) BUT IF YOU LAND ON THE HEAD OF A SNAKE YOU MUST SLIDE BACK DOWN TO ITS TAIL (UNLUCKY!). NOW PASS THE DICE ON TO THE NEXT PLAYER.

4. TO WIN THE GAME, ONE PLAYER MUST LAND EXACTLY ON SQUARE 90. IF YOU ROLL TOO HIGH THEN YOU HAVE TO MOVE BOTH FORWARDS AND BACKWARDS TO COMPLETE YOUR TURN. (FOR EXAMPLE, IF YOU ARE ON SQUARE 88 AND ROLL A 3, YOU MUST MOVE FORWARD TWO SPACES TO 90 AND THEN BACK ONE SPACE IN ORDER TO FULFIL THE THREE MOVES).

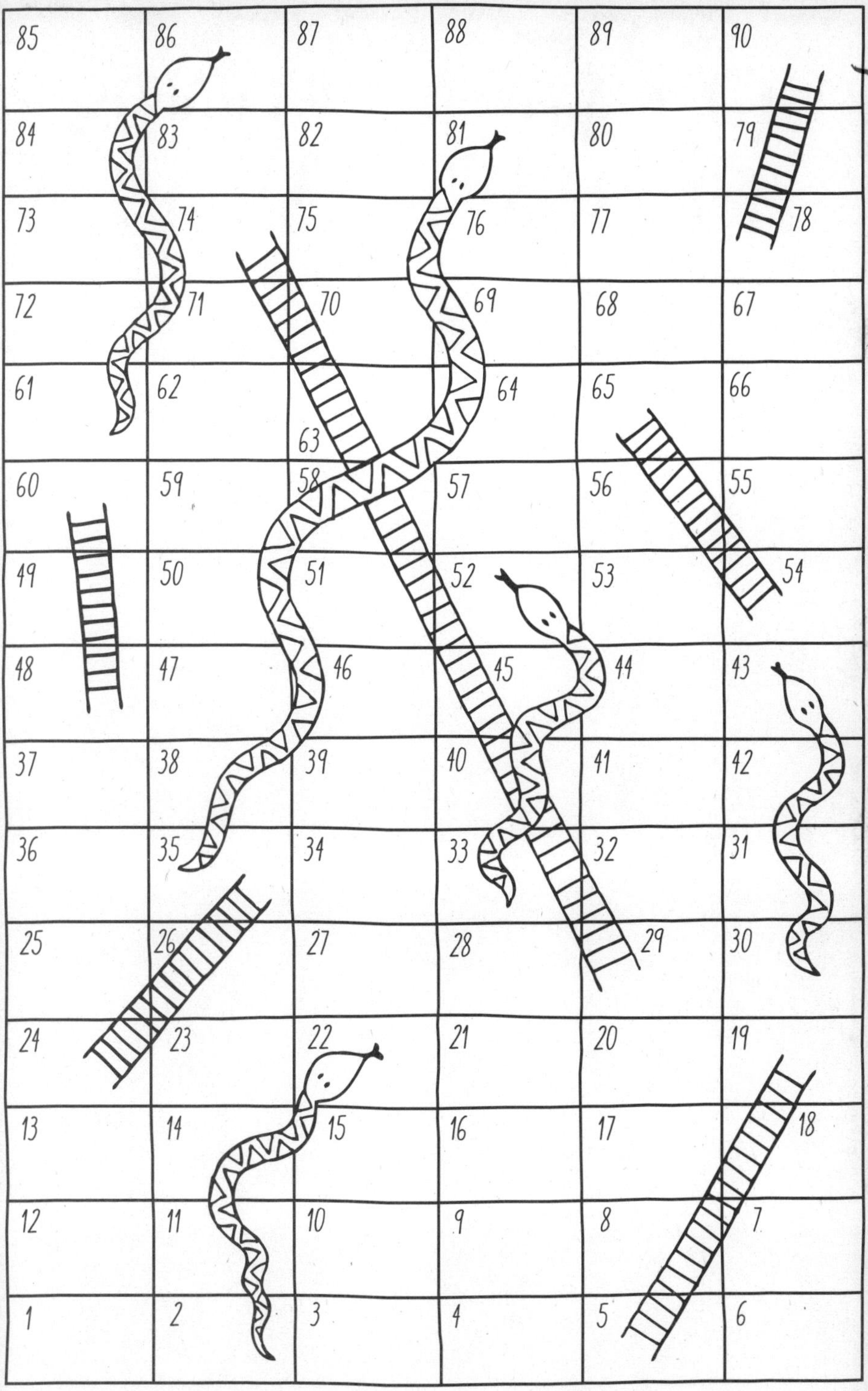
85 86 87 88 89 90
84 83 82 81 80 79
73 74 75 76 77 78
72 71 70 69 68 67
61 62 63 64 65 66
60 59 58 57 56 55
49 50 51 52 53 54
48 47 46 45 44 43
37 38 39 40 41 42
36 35 34 33 32 31
25 26 27 28 29 30
24 23 22 21 20 19
13 14 15 16 17 18
12 11 10 9 8 7
1 2 3 4 5 6

GET YOUR FRIENDS TO SIGN THIS PAGE

TONGUE TWISTERS

TRY SAYING THESE REALLY QUICKLY:

I SCREAM, YOU SCREAM, WE ALL SCREAM
FOR ICE CREAM!

GOBBLING GARGOYLES GOBBLED GOBBLING
GOBLINS.

HOW MUCH WOOD COULD CHUCK WOODS'
WOODCHUCK CHUCK, IF CHUCK WOODS'
WOODCHUCK COULD AND WOULD CHUCK WOOD?
IF CHUCK WOODS' WOODCHUCK COULD AND
WOULD CHUCK WOOD, HOW MUCH WOOD COULD
AND WOULD CHUCK WOODS' WOODCHUCK
CHUCK? CHUCK WOODS' WOODCHUCK WOULD
CHUCK, HE WOULD, AS MUCH AS HE COULD,
AND CHUCK AS MUCH WOOD AS ANY
WOODCHUCK WOULD, IF A WOODCHUCK COULD
AND WOULD CHUCK WOOD.

THE BOOK ON YOUR HEAD CHALLENGE

A SELF PORTRAIT

PUT YOUR POINTLESS 2 BOOK ON YOUR HEAD (NOT NOW, WAIT UNTIL YOU READ ALL THE INSTRUCTIONS FIRST!). GRAB A PEN AND DRAW THE FOLLOWING IMAGES ON THE PAGE WHILST HOLDING THE BOOK ON YOUR HEAD!

A FLOWER

POINTLESS FACTS

YOU BREATHE ON AVERAGE ABOUT FIVE MILLION TIMES A YEAR.

THE AVERAGE PERSON SPENDS TWO WEEKS OF THEIR LIFETIME WAITING FOR THE LIGHT TO CHANGE FROM RED TO GREEN.

YOUR LEFT LUNG IS SMALLER THAN YOUR RIGHT LUNG TO MAKE ROOM FOR YOUR HEART.

CHEWING GUM WHILE PEELING ONIONS WILL STOP YOU FROM CRYING.

THE OLDEST KNOWN GOLDFISH LIVED TO 43 YEARS OF AGE. HER NAME WAS TISH.

THE STRAW FOOTBALL GAME

LET'S PLAY SOME STRAW FOOTBALL! HERE'S HOW TO PLAY:

1. YOU'LL SEE THERE ARE TWO RECTANGLES ON THIS PAGE. CUT THEM OUT AND ROLL THEM LENGTHWAYS – THESE ARE YOUR STRAWS!

2. YOU'LL ALSO SEE THERE IS A CIRCLE ON THIS PAGE TOO. CUT THIS OUT AND ROLL IT INTO A BALL. THIS WILL BE YOUR, ERM, BALL!

3. ON THE PAGE OPPOSITE THERE ARE TWO GOALS. RIP THE PAGE OUT AND PLAY STRAW FOOTBALL WITH A FRIEND!

- - - - - - - - - - - - - - - -

CUT HERE

- - - - - - - - - - - - - - - -

CUT HERE

- - - - - - - - - - - - - - - -

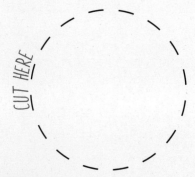

CUT HERE

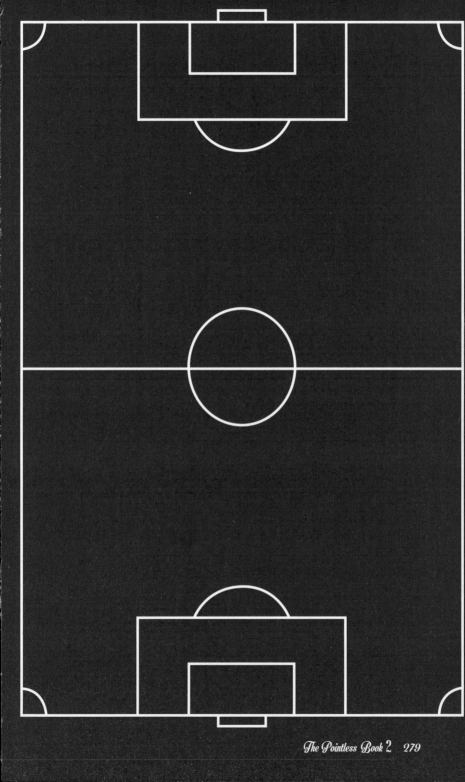

DESIGN YOUR LAPTOP BACK

DRAW AN AMAZING DESIGN ON THE BACK OF THE LAPTOP!

SODA PONG!

SODA PONG IS THE BEST GAME EVER.
FOR THIS GAME YOU WILL NEED:

SCAN HERE
TO SEE
ALFIE'S
ATTEMPTS

PB2

1. A FRIEND

2. 12 PLASTIC CUPS

3. A PING PONG BALL « ○ ”

4. A CARTON OF ORANGE JUICE

5. GRAVY GRANULES AND WATER (TO MAKE GRAVY!)

INSTRUCTIONS:

GRAB THE CUPS AND DIVIDE THEM INTO TWO GROUPS OF SIX.

IN SIX CUPS POUR A SPLASH OF ORANGE JUICE AND IN THE OTHER
SIX ADD A SPLASH OF GRAVY.

MIX UP THE CUPS AND PLACE SIX AT ONE END OF A TABLE
AND SIX AT ANOTHER END. THE AIM OF THE GAME IS TO
BOUNCE THE PING PONG BALL INTO A CUP AND THE OPPONENT
HAS TO DRINK WHATEVER IS IN THE CUP!

TWEETING RARITIES!

TWEET PICTURES TO #POINTLESSPICS WHEN YOU SEE THE FOLLOWING...

A WHITE PIGEON

ALFIE DEYES

A PINK CAR

A MAN ON A UNICYCLE

SOMEBODY WITH THE POINTLESS BOOK 2

A BRIGHT GREEN BUILDING

SOMEONE WITH POINTLESS BLOG MERCHANDISE

TO DO LIST

CATCHPHRASES

GUESS THE NAME OF THE SONG FROM
THE VISUAL CLUES BELOW...

1.

2.

_____   _____

3.

4.

_____   _____

SPECIAL BIRTHDAYS

NAME: _____

DATE: _____

WHAT DID YOU DO? _____

_____

NAME: _____

DATE: _____

WHAT DID YOU DO? _____

_____

NAME: _____

DATE: _____

WHAT DID YOU DO? _____

_____

NAME: _____

DATE: _____

WHAT DID YOU DO? _____

_____

WHAT ARE YOUR MOST PRIZED POSSESSIONS?

DRAW OR LIST THEM HERE:

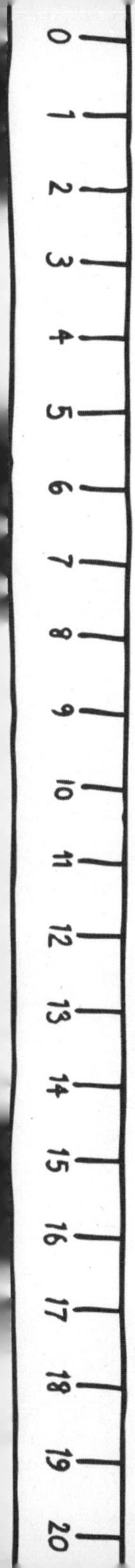
0
1
2
3
4
5
6
7
8
9
10
11
12
13
14
15
16
17
18
19
20

RULER REACTIONS

GRAB A RULER AND TEST YOUR REACTIONS. ASK A FRIEND TO HOLD THE RULER LENGTHWAYS AND IN THE AIR. PLACE YOUR FINGERS AROUND THE RULER, BUT NOT TOUCHING IT. THE AIM IS TO CATCH THE RULER BETWEEN YOUR FINGERS AS SOON AS YOUR FRIEND DROPS IT AND TO MEASURE YOUR REACTIONS USING THE RULER.

PERSONAL BESTS:

1. ____________CM
2. ____________CM
3. ____________CM
4. ____________CM
5. ____________CM

0–5	WAKEY! WAKEY! HAVE ANOTHER TRY...
6–10	SHARP, BUT NOT SHARP ENOUGH...
11–15	OK, THAT'S PRETTY IMPRESSIVE...
16–20	WOW! HELLO SPEEDY GONZALEZ!

PAINTING BY NUMBERS

PAINT THE PICTURE USING THE NUMBERS AND COLOURS BELOW.

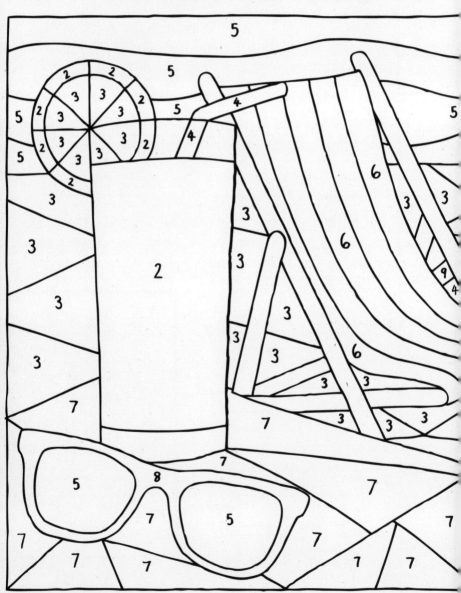

MAKE AN ALFIE FACE WITH YOUR FOOD...

EVERYONE LIKES PLAYING WITH THEIR FOOD! NOW YOU CAN PLAY WITH YOUR FOOD AND TWEET IT TO

#POINTLESSFOOD

MAKE ALFIE'S FACE OUT OF YOUR FAVOURITE DINNER AND TWEET AWAY!

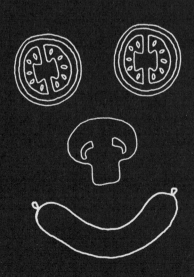

TREASURE HUNT

CREATE YOUR OWN TREASURE HUNT TO DO WITH YOUR FRIENDS! HIDE THIS BOOK SOMEWHERE SAFE AND WRITE DOWN CLUES FOR THEM TO FOLLOW IN ORDER TO FIND IT. KEEP HOLD OF CLUE ONE (THEY'LL NEED THAT TO START THE HUNT) AND HIDE THE REST IN DIFFERENT SPOTS FOR THEM TO FIND – REMEMBER, CLUE 1 SHOULD LEAD TO CLUE 2, AND SO ON!

CLUE 1

CLUE 2

CLUE 3

CLUE 4

CLUE 5

CREATE YOUR OWN CARTOON CHARACTER!

GRAB A PICTURE OF YOURSELF AND DRAW A CARTOON CHARACTER. EXAGGERATE YOUR FEATURES AND BE CREATIVE!

SCAN HERE TO SEE ALFIE'S CARTOON

PB2

DESIGN A T-SHIRT

HERE'S ANOTHER DESIGN ACTIVITY. ADD AN AMAZING DESIGN TO THE T-SHIRT BELOW; YOU CAN ADD WHATEVER YOU LIKE – JUST BE CREATIVE!

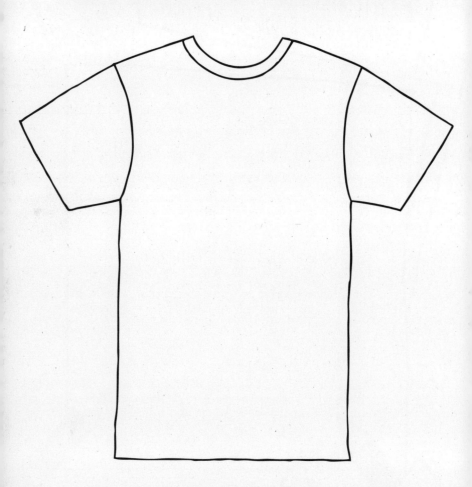

CREATE YOUR OWN ULTIMATE CHOCOLATE BAR!

EVERYONE LOVES CHOCOLATE. NOW'S YOUR CHANCE TO DESIGN YOUR VERY OWN CHOCOLATE BAR! WE'VE STARTED OFF THE DESIGN BELOW...

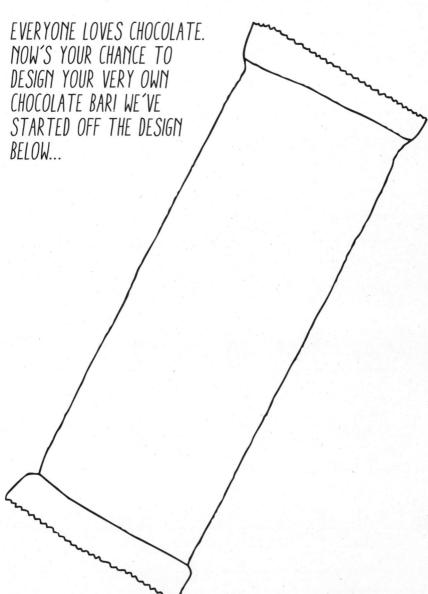

DREAM JOURNAL

LAST NIGHT I DREAMT: _____
_____
_____
_____
_____
_____
_____
_____
_____
_____
_____
_____
_____
_____
_____
_____
_____
_____
_____

I THINK THIS MEANS: _____
_____
_____
_____
_____
_____
_____

CUT-OUT LOVEHEARTS

EVER WANTED TO TELL SOMEONE HOW YOU REALLY FEEL ABOUT THEM BUT NEVER KNEW WHAT TO SAY? NOW'S YOUR CHANCE! JUST DECORATE THE LOVEHEARTS BELOW, CUT THEM OUT AND PASS THEM ON.

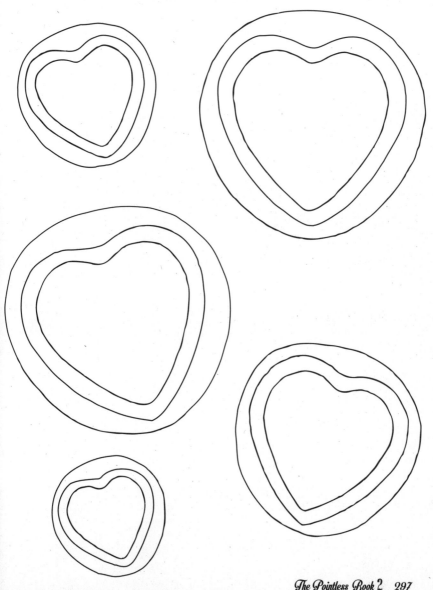

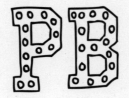

THE 'YES' AND 'NO' GAME

SCAN HERE TO SEE ALFIE'S ATTEMPTS

PB2

GRAB A FRIEND AND PLAY THE 'YES' AND 'NO' GAME.

HERE'S HOW TO PLAY:

PLAYER 1 THINKS OF A FAMOUS PERSON.

PLAYER 2 ASKS PLAYER 1 A SERIES OF QUESTIONS. PLAYER 1 HAS TO ANSWER THE QUESTIONS WITHOUT SAYING 'YES' OR 'NO'!

EACH PLAYER RECORDS THEIR TIME AND THE WINNER IS THE PLAYER WHO HAS LASTED THE LONGEST WITHOUT SAYING 'YES' OR 'NO'!

PLAYER 1	PLAYER 2

PIN THE TAIL ON NALA

EVERYONE REMEMBERS 'PIN THE TAIL ON THE DONKEY' FROM THEIR CHILDHOOD — SO LET'S PLAY A GAME OF 'PIN THE TAIL ON NALA'!

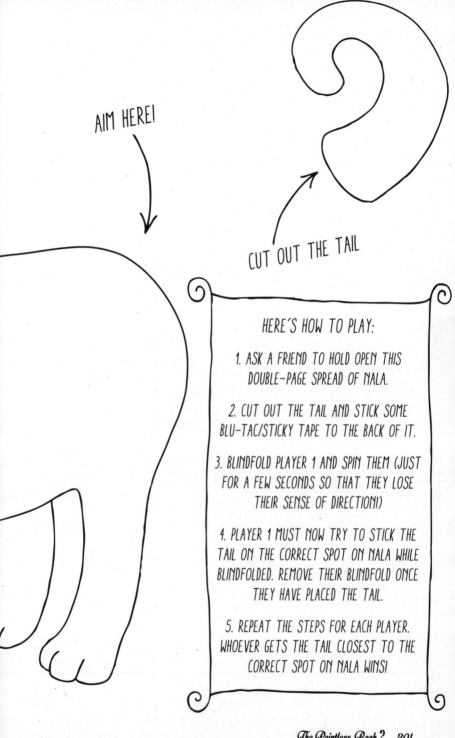

AIM HERE!

CUT OUT THE TAIL

HERE'S HOW TO PLAY:

1. ASK A FRIEND TO HOLD OPEN THIS DOUBLE-PAGE SPREAD OF NALA.

2. CUT OUT THE TAIL AND STICK SOME BLU-TAC/STICKY TAPE TO THE BACK OF IT.

3. BLINDFOLD PLAYER 1 AND SPIN THEM (JUST FOR A FEW SECONDS SO THAT THEY LOSE THEIR SENSE OF DIRECTION!)

4. PLAYER 1 MUST NOW TRY TO STICK THE TAIL ON THE CORRECT SPOT ON NALA WHILE BLINDFOLDED. REMOVE THEIR BLINDFOLD ONCE THEY HAVE PLACED THE TAIL.

5. REPEAT THE STEPS FOR EACH PLAYER. WHOEVER GETS THE TAIL CLOSEST TO THE CORRECT SPOT ON NALA WINS!

DESIGN YOUR OWN MENU

BREAKFAST

LUNCH

DINNER

DESSERT

MIRROR WRITING

CHECK OUT THE IMAGES BELOW. GRAB A MIRROR
AND WRITE WHAT YOU SEE...

DO MORE OF WHAT
MAKES YOU HAPPY!

NAIA IS THE COOLEST
DOG IN THE WORLD!

SORRY ABOUT MY
HAIR!

YOU DON'T HAVE TO
DO WHAT EVERYONE
ELSE IS DOING!

Fishing

_____

_____

_____

_____

MAKE SOCK PUPPETS

OKAY POINTLESS PEOPLE, IT'S TIME TO GET CREATIVE
WITH YOUR, ERM, SOCKS!

WHAT YOU NEED:

ONE LONELY UNPAIRED SOCK
CRAFT GLUE
TWO BUTTONS FOR THE EYES
SOME WOOL

INSTRUCTIONS:

1. FIRST PUT THE SOCK ON YOUR HAND SO THAT
YOUR FINGERS ARE IN THE TOE SECTION AND YOUR
THUMB IS IN THE HEEL SECTION. MARK WHERE YOU'D
LIKE THE EYES TO BE.

2. NEXT, GLUE THE BUTTONS TO THE SOCK AT
THE POINTS WHERE YOU MARKED THE EYES.
(BE CAREFUL NOT TO SPILL ANY GLUE!)

3. NOW FOR THE HAIR! CUT THE WOOL INTO A COOL
HAIRSTYLE FOR YOUR PUPPET AND GLUE IT ON.

CONGRATULATIONS! YOU NOW HAVE YOUR VERY OWN SOCK PUPPET!

DRAW NALA'S BALL

NALA LOVES HER BALL; IT'S HER FAVOURITE TOY. DESIGN NALA'S BALL IN THE SPACE BELOW, MAKING IT AS DECORATIVE AS YOU LIKE!

MAKE SURE YOU DRAW WITHIN THE LINES!

SCAN HERE TO SEE YOUR DESIGN

PB2

POINTLESS FLOWCHART

HIDE AND SEEK

GET YOUR FRIEND TO
HIDE YOUR BOOK AND
SEE HOW LONG IT TAKES
YOU TO FIND IT.

TIME:

DECORATE NALA'S BACKGROUND

THIS IS THE ULTIMATE CHALLENGE. COLOUR IN NALA'S BACKGROUND!

WRITE DOWN YOUR TOP FIVE FAVOURITE EVER TEXTS:

1. _____
   _____

2. _____
   _____

3. _____
   _____

4. _____
   _____

5. _____
   _____

DRAW YOUR FAVOURITE VIDEO OR FILM SCENE (COMIC BOOK STYLE)

GRATITUDE WEEK

WRITE DOWN SOMETHING YOU ARE GRATEFUL FOR
EVERY DAY OF THE WEEK.

MONDAY: _____

_____

_____

TUESDAY: _____

_____

_____

WEDNESDAY: _____

_____

_____

THURSDAY: _____
_____
_____

FRIDAY: _____
_____
_____

SATURDAY: _____
_____
_____

SUNDAY: _____
_____
_____

THE POINTLESS PRIZE PAGE!

EVERYONE DESERVES A PRIZE FROM TIME TO TIME. ON THIS PAGE, LIST
TEN REASONS WHY YOU DESERVE A POINTLESS PRIZE AND THEN WRITE
WHAT YOU THINK THAT PRIZE SHOULD BE!

1. _____

2. _____

3. _____

4. _____

5. _____

6. _____

7. _____

8. _____

9. _____

10. _____

THE PRIZE: _____

POINTLESS POETRY

YOU'RE A POET AND YOU KNOW IT! USE THE WORDS BELOW TO MAKE SOME POINTLESS POETRY! TWEET YOUR VERSE TO #POINTLESSPOETRY...

PUG
FUDGE
RAINBOW
CROISSANT
BUBBLE
CHEEKY
EMOJI
SUNSHINE
HAPPY
TOOTHPASTE
SMELLY
CHICKEN
MOONWALK
FIFTY
PEANUT
BUTTER
TWEET

ALFIE'S DICTIONARY CHALLENGE!

OK WORD WORMS, HERE IS A LIST OF OBSCURE WORDS.
TRY TO MATCH THEM WITH THE ANSWERS BELOW!

WORDS

1. BOONDOGGLE

2. CYGNET

3. GUMPTION

4. KALOOKI

5. OSCULATE

6. WIDDERSHINS

7. TALIPOT

8. HORNSWOGGLE

ANSWERS

A. TO CHEAT OR TRICK

B. COMMON SENSE

C. MOVE COUNTER CLOCKWISE

D. A YOUNG SWAN

E. A PALM TREE

F. A FORM OF RUMMY PLAYED
WITH TWO PACKS OF CARD

G. AN UNNECESSARY EXPERIENCE

H. TO KISS

THE POINTLESS PONDER PAGE

STOP HERE AND HAVE A THINK ABOUT THE FOLLOWING...

IN THE CINEMA, WHICH ARM REST IS YOURS?

IF AN AMBULANCE IS ON ITS WAY TO SAVE SOMEONE AND IT RUNS SOMEONE OVER, DOES IT STOP TO SAVE THEM OR CONTINUE TO THE FIRST PERSON?

ONE RAINDROP PLUS ANOTHER RAINDROP MAKES ONE RAINDROP?

WHY DOES A ROUND PIZZA COME IN A SQUARE BOX?

IF YOU PUT A CHAMELEON IN A ROOM FULL OF MIRRORS, WHAT COLOUR WOULD IT TURN?

IF NOBODY BUYS A TICKET TO A FILM, DO THEY STILL SHOW IT?

DOES THE POSTMAN DELIVER HIS OWN MAIL?

WHY DOESN'T SUPERGLUE STICK TO THE INSIDE OF THE TUBE?

CHOOSE 5 WORDS BELOW THAT BEST DESCRIBE YOU

FRIENDLY

KIND

AWKWARD

SILLY

FIERY

TALKATIVE

LOUD

CREATIVE

PRACTICAL

FRANTIC

LAZY

PROACTIVE

MUSICAL

SPORTY

TRUSTWORTHY

QUIET

GULLIBLE

FIDGETY

DREAMY

PERFECTIONIST

POSITIVE

INDEPENDENT

EMOTIONAL

LEADER

PARTICULAR

CANDID

OUTSPOKEN

HONEST

COMMITTED

KNOWLEDGEABLE

LOGICAL

COMPASSIONATE

CHEERFUL

PATIENT

FORGIVING

REBELLIOUS

UNDERSTANDING

ACHIEVER

THOUGHTFUL

QUIRKY

PERSISTENT

SOCIABLE

HARD WORKER

GENEROUS

FAVOURITES

CHOOSE YOUR FAVOURITE...

SWEET POPCORN OR SALTED POPCORN?

BIRTHDAY OR CHRISTMAS?

KITTENS OR PUPPIES?

PIZZA OR BURGER?

SUMMER OR WINTER?

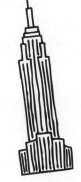

TWITTER OR INSTAGRAM?

YOUTUBE OR TV?

NEW YORK OR PARIS?

FRUIT OR VEG?

SCAN HERE TO SEE ALFIE'S FAVOURITES

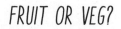

RIDDLE

SIX GLASSES ARE PLACED IN A ROW.

THE FIRST THREE CONTAIN WATER; THE SECOND THREE ARE EMPTY.

BY MOVING ONLY ONE GLASS, HOW IS IT POSSIBLE TO REARRANGE THE GLASSES SO THEY ALTERNATE BETWEEN FULL AND EMPTY?

ANSWER: _____

_____

BEGINNING OF THE WEEK RESOLUTIONS

DATE: _____

RESOLUTION: _____

_____

_____

_____

DATE: _____

RESOLUTION: _____

_____

_____

_____

DATE: _____

RESOLUTION: _____

_____

_____

_____

DATE: _____

RESOLUTION: _____

_____

_____

_____

SPOT THE DIFFERENCE...

DOT TO DOT

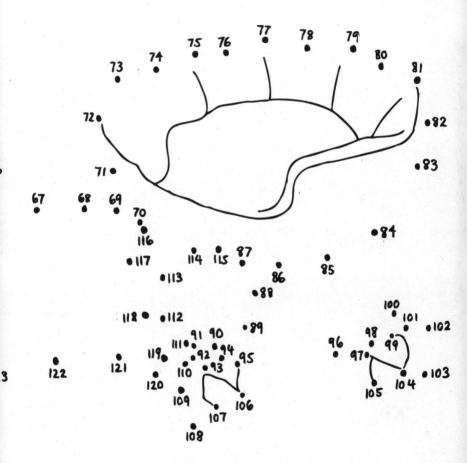

SPIN THE BOOK

GATHER SOME FRIENDS AND PLAY A GAME OF 'SPIN THE BOOK'. HERE'S HOW TO PLAY:

1. ON THE OPPOSITE PAGE WRITE A DARE IN EACH OF THE FIVE BOXES.

2. CUT OUT THE DARES.

3. CLOSE YOUR POINTLESS BOOK (BUT READ ALL OF THE INSTRUCTIONS FIRST).

4. SIT IN A CIRCLE WITH YOUR FRIENDS AND PLACE EACH DARE AROUND THE CIRCLE.

5. TURN OVER YOUR POINTLESS BOOK AND LOOK FOR THE SPECIAL ARROW.

6. TAKE IT IN TURNS TO SPIN YOUR POINTLESS BOOK.

7. IF THE ARROW STOPS ON A DARE, YOU HAVE TO PERFORM THE DARE.

8. IF IT MISSES A DARE, THEN THE BOOK IS PASSED ON TO THE NEXT PLAYER FOR THEIR TURN.

DARE 1

DARE 2

DARE 3

DARE 4

DARE 5

TABLE TENNIS

LET'S PLAY A GAME OF TABLE TENNIS – BUT WITH A TWIST.

HERE'S HOW TO PLAY:

1. YOU NEED AN OPPONENT SO GRAB A FRIEND WHO WOULD LIKE TO PLAY.

2. TEAR OUT THIS PAGE (NOT YET – READ ALL THE INSTRUCTIONS FIRST!).

3. SCRUNCH UP THE PAGE INTO A BALL. THIS IS YOUR PING PONG BALL.

4. CLOSE THE POINTLESS BOOK 2 AND PLACE IT ON ITS SIDE IN THE MIDDLE OF A TABLE (IF YOUR FRIEND HAS A POINTLESS BOOK 2 THEN YOU CAN USE THAT TOO!). THIS IS YOUR NET.

5. THE AIM OF THE GAME IS TO BOUNCE THE BALL OVER THE NET AND LAND IT ON THE OTHER SIDE OF THE TABLE.

6. THE WINNER IS THE PLAYER WHO SCORES THE MOST 'LANDINGS' AFTER TEN ATTEMPTS EACH.

CELEBRITY LINK GAME

THIS GAME IS SO MUCH FUN, ESPECIALLY IF YOU'RE TRYING TO PASS THE TIME. THE AIM OF THE GAME IS TO LINK CELEBRITIES USING THE FINAL LETTER OF THEIR NAMES. FOR EXAMPLE, EMMA WATSO<u>N</u> CAN BE LINKED TO <u>N</u>IALL HORA<u>N</u>, AND THEN <u>N</u>IALL HORA<u>N</u> CAN BE LINKED TO <u>N</u>ICKI MINA<u>J</u>... TRY IT WITH THE NAMES BELOW!

JUSTIN BIEBER

HARRY STYLES

GRAPH PAPER

FINISH THE TEXT CONVERSATION

'WAIT... SAID WHAT?!'

'I CAN'T BELIEVE HE ACTUALLY SAID THAT TO HER!!'

DOODLES

...FILL THIS PAGE WITH DOODLES!

GET YOUR FRIEND TO FILL THIS PAGE

PASS YOUR BOOK TO A FRIEND AND GET THEM TO FILL IN THIS PAGE

DRAW...

THE DESCRIPTION BELOW ON THE OPPOSITE PAGE AND
SHARE USING #POINTLESSPICTURE...

ALFIE AND NALA WALKING ON THE MOON,
ALONGSIDE A POINTLESS FLAG AND A POINTLESS
SPACECRAFT. BE CREATIVE AND INCLUDE AS MUCH
DETAIL AS YOU LIKE – SUCH AS A FEW STARS,
THE SUN, EARTH, ANOTHER SPACECRAFT, A
FEW ALIENS, A COUPLE OF METEORS, A FEW OF
ALFIE'S FRIENDS, AND MAYBE EVEN A BLACK HOLE!
DON'T FORGET TO TWEET YOUR PICTURE TO
#POINTLESSPICTURE.

POINTLESS CHECKLIST

WRITE A CHECKLIST FOR TODAY AND TICK IT OFF AS YOU COMPLETE EACH ONE!

- ☐
- ☐
- ☐
- ☐
- ☐
- ☐
- ☐
- ☐
- ☐
- ☐
- ☐
- ☐
- ☐
- ☐
- ☐
- ☐
- ☐
- ☐
- ☐
- ☐

FAVOURITE WEBSITES

_____

_____

_____

_____

_____

_____

_____

SPY ON PEOPLE

...WHAT DID YOU SEE?

STICK A CHILDHOOD PHOTO HERE

SCAN HERE TO SEE ALFIE'S PHOTO

PB2

ADD YOUR PHOTO WITHIN THE LINES

BEST EVER STATUSES

☐ _____
   _____

☐ _____
   _____

☐ _____
   _____

☐ _____
   _____

☐ _____
   _____

PALM READING

LET'S TRY SOME PALM READING AND SEE IF WE CAN LOOK INTO THE FUTURE...

THE HEART LINE
IF YOUR HEART LINE IS TOUCHING YOUR LIFE LINE THIS COULD MEAN THAT YOUR HEART CAN BE EASILY BROKEN; IF IT IS PARALLEL TO YOUR LIFE LINE, THOUGH, THEN YOU ARE IN CONTROL OF YOUR EMOTIONS!

THE HEAD LINE
IS YOUR HEAD LINE STRAIGHT AND LONG? THIS SUGGESTS THAT YOU THINK CLEARLY AND SENSIBLY! OR IS IT CURVED? THIS COULD MEAN YOU ARE CREATIVE AND OPEN TO NEW IDEAS!

THE FATE LINE
DO YOU HAVE A PROMINENT FATE LINE? THIS SUGGESTS THAT YOU ARE CONTROLLED BY DESTINY! DOES IT ALSO START AT THE BASE OF YOUR PALM? THIS COULD MEAN THAT YOU WILL FIND YOUR WAY INTO THE PUBLIC EYE!

THE LIFE LINE
(DON'T WORRY, THIS ISN'T AN INDICATOR OF HOW LONG YOU LIVE!)

ARE THERE BREAKS IN YOUR LIFE LINE? THIS IMPLIES THAT YOU WILL EXPERIENCE GREAT CHANGE IN YOUR LIFETIME! OR IS IT CLOSE TO THE EDGE OF YOUR PALM? THIS CAN MEAN THAT YOU ARE A CAUTIOUS PERSON!

THE HEART LINE   THE HEAD LINE
THE FATE LINE   THE LIFE LINE

FUNNIEST OVERHEARD CONVERSATIONS ON A BUS OR A TRAIN

SECRET KEY

THIS WAY UP!

YOU'VE FOUND THE SECRET KEY!
NOW, CUT OUT THE SQUARE ON THE
DOTTED LINES AND FIND THE BOX
THAT NEEDS TO BE UNLOCKED...

RIP THIS PAGE...

...INTO PIECES AND STICK IT BACK TOGETHER TO MAKE THIS CIRCLE

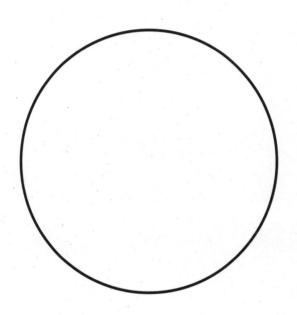

DRAW A COFFEE CUP

DESIGN YOUR COFFEE CUP IN THE SPACE BELOW, MAKING IT AS DECORATIVE AS YOU LIKE!

MAKE SURE YOU DRAW WITHIN THE LINES!

SCAN HERE TO SEE YOUR DESIGN

PB2

TIMELINE OF YOUR LIFE

USE THE LINE BELOW TO PLOT A TIMELINE OF YOUR LIFE.
BEGIN WITH YOUR DATE OF BIRTH AND BE AS CREATIVE AS
YOU WISH! YOU COULD EVEN PLOT INTO THE FUTURE...

ADD YOUR DATE OF
BIRTH HERE!

DRAW OR LIST ALL THE THINGS

SPRING

SUMMER

THAT REMIND YOU OF...

AUTUMN

WINTER

CLOUD HUNTERS

TICK OFF THESE CLOUD TYPES
WHEN YOU SPOT THEM:

CIRROCUMULUS

☐

DATE: _____

CUMULONIMBUS

☐

DATE: _____

CIRRUS

☐

DATE: _____

ALTOCUMULUS

☐

DATE: _____

STRATOCUMULUS

☐

DATE: _____

STRATUS

☐

DATE: _____

NIMBOSTRATUS

☐

DATE: _____

SWITCH OFF THIS LIGHT

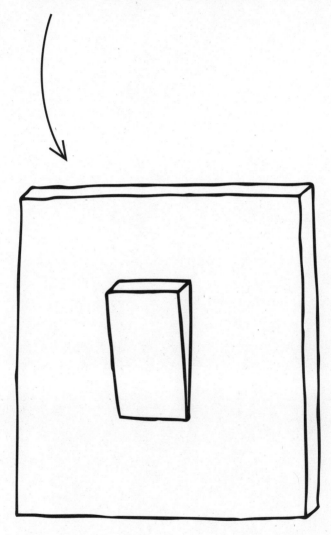

NOW HOW DO YOU

SWITCH IT BACK ON?

WRITE DOWN THE MOST EXCITING THINGS HAPPENING THIS YEAR

STICK ALL YOUR CINEMA TICKETS HERE AND RATE EACH FILM

☆☆☆☆☆

☆☆☆☆☆

☆☆☆☆☆

☆☆☆☆☆

☆☆☆☆☆

LIFE HACKS

CHECK OUT THESE AMAZING LIFE HACKS...

HERE'S HOW TO BUILD A SOFA FORT, JUST IN CASE YOU EVER NEED TO:

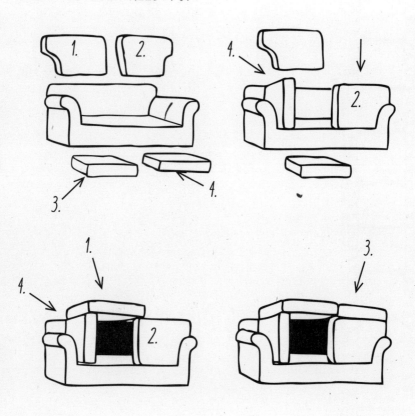

HOW TO MAKE AN ICE CREAM COOKIE SANDWICH:

YOU'LL NEED A TUB OF VANILLA ICE CREAM AND SOME COOKIES.

WITH A KNIFE*, CUT A SLICE OUT OF YOUR TUB.

GRAB YOUR COOKIES.

PLACE THE SLICE BETWEEN THE TWO COOKIES.

PEEL OFF THE TUB'S CARDBOARD...

...AND YOU HAVE AN ICE CREAM COOKIE SANDWICH!

HOW TO MAKE A HANDS-FREE POPCORN HOLDER:

WEAR A HOODIE BACK TO FRONT AND POUR IN YOUR POPCORN!

SCAN HERE TO SEE ALFIE IN ACTION

PB2

*ASK AN ADULT IF YOU ARE UNDER 16

The Pointless Book 2   363

POINTLESS PREDICTIONS FOR THIS YEAR

YOUR 3 PREDICTIONS:

1. _____
_____
_____
_____

2. _____
_____
_____
_____

3. _____
_____
_____
_____

YOUR FRIEND'S 3 PREDICTIONS:

1. _____
_____
_____
_____

2. _____
_____
_____
_____

3. _____
_____
_____
_____

GLUE HERE

LOCK THIS PAGE

SEAL HERE

...AND OPEN IT IN 12 MONTHS!

SECRET SWAPPING

WRITE DOWN A SECRET HERE AND SWAP
YOUR BOOK WITH A FRIEND TO SHARE THEM

MAKE THIS
PAGE SPARKLY!

CUPCAKE FULL ENGLISH

CUPCAKES. BREAKFAST. TWO OF THE GREATEST THINGS IN THE WORLD! LET'S COMBINE THE TWO AND MAKE A SCRUMPTIOUS CUPCAKE FULL ENGLISH! HERE ARE THE INSTRUCTIONS:

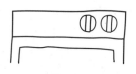

1. PRE-HEAT THE OVEN TO 200°C.*

2. GRAB SOME BREAD AND A CUPCAKE TRAY.

3. DAB A LITTLE OIL INTO EACH CUP.

4. CUT THE BREAD INTO ENOUGH CIRCLES FOR YOUR TRAY AND PLACE IN EACH CUP.

5. MEANWHILE BROWN SOME BACON IN A FRYING PAN.*

6. WRAP THE BROWNED BACON AROUND THE INSIDE OF EACH CUP AND BAKE FOR 10 MINUTES.

7. SCRAMBLE SOME EGGS IN A SEPARATE DISH AND POUR INTO THE CUPCAKE TRAY HOLES. DON'T FORGET TO SPRINKLE SOME CHEESE TOO!

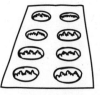

8. BAKE FOR ANOTHER 10 MINUTES UNTIL THE EGG IS SET AND THE CHEESE HAS MELTED.

9. ENJOY!

*ASK AN ADULT IF YOU ARE UNDER 16

POINTLESS
BOOK SELFIE

GRAB A COPY OF YOUR POINTLESS
BOOK AND TAKE A SELFIE!

TWEET TO
#POINTLESSBOOKSELFIE

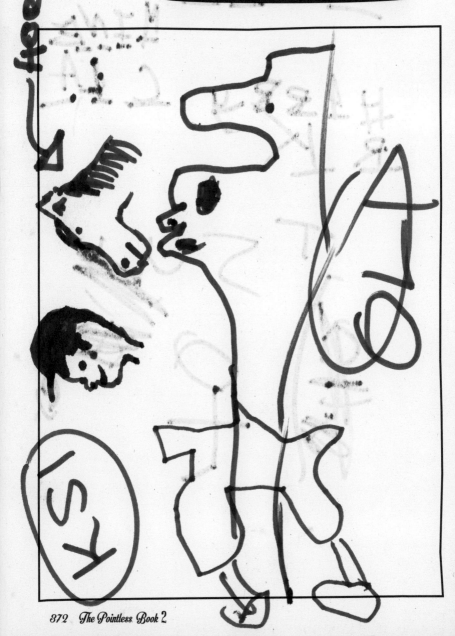

5 NEW FOODS

SCAN HERE TO REVEAL ALFIE'S CHOICES

PB2

TRY 5 FOODS YOU'VE NEVER TRIED BEFORE AND LIST THEM HERE. WHAT WAS EACH ONE LIKE?

1. _____

_____

2. _____

_____

3. _____

_____

4. _____

_____

5. _____

_____

CHUBBY BUNNY CHALLENGE

HERE'S A CLASSIC: THE CHUBBY BUNNY CHALLENGE. FOR THIS GAME YOU'LL NEED:

A PACKET OF MARSHMALLOWS.

MAYBE A COUPLE OF FRIENDS TO LAUGH AT YOU.

HERE'S HOW TO PLAY:

1. PUT A MARSHMALLOW IN YOUR MOUTH.

2. SAY 'CHUBBY BUNNY'.

3. PUT ANOTHER MARSHMALLOW IN YOUR MOUTH.

4. SAY 'CHUBBY BUNNY'.

5. PUT A MARSHMALLOW IN YOUR MOUTH.

6. SAY 'CHUBBY BUNNY'.

7. PUT ANOTHER MARSHMALLOW IN YOUR MOUTH.

8. SAY 'CHUBBY BUNNY'.

9. KEEP GOING UNTIL YOU CAN'T SAY 'CHUBBY BUNNY'.

DO MORE OF WHAT MAKES YOU HAPPY

IF YOU HAD A PUG WHAT WOULD YOU CALL IT?

TRUE OR FALSE?

THE COLOUR ORANGE IS NAMED AFTER THE FRUIT. ☐ ☐

GOOGLE WAS ORIGINALLY CALLED 'BACKRUB'. ☐ ☐

HUMAN HAIR AND FINGERNAILS CONTINUE TO GROW AFTER DEATH. ☐ ☐

THERE ARE 86,400 SECONDS IN A DAY. ☐ ☐

HUMANS SHARE 90% OF THEIR DNA WITH BANANAS. ☐ ☐

IT IS IMPOSSIBLE TO BREATHE AND SWALLOW AT THE SAME TIME. ☐ ☐

DRAW FROM MEMORY...

WITH A FRIEND, LOOK AT THE PICTURE BELOW FOR FIVE SECONDS AND COVER IT UP. TRY TO DRAW THE PICTURE FROM MEMORY ON THE OPPOSITE PAGE AND SEE WHO REMEMBERS THE MOST!

YOU

RI IS HOT
'VE F M NQB

YOUR FRIEND

I wish P WAS MINE

a C D F G J K L O
R T U V X Y

ANSWER PAGES

POINTLESS RIDDLES

PAGE 208

1. WIND

2. TWELVE! JANUARY 2ND; FEBRUARY 2ND ETC...

3. AN UMBRELLA

4. A WINDOW

TRANSLATION PAGE

PAGE 264

1. CHINESE

2. GERMAN

3. ITALIAN

4. GREEK

5. FRENCH

6. SPANISH

CATCHPHRASES

PAGE 284

1. SING BY ED SHEERAN

2. STEAL MY GIRL BY ONE DIRECTION

3. GHOST BY ELLA HENDERSON

4. HAPPY BY PHARRELL WILLIAMS

DICTIONARY CHALLENGE

PAGE 318

1 – G

2 – D

3 – B

4 – F

5 – H

6 – C

7 – E

8 – A

CUP RIDDLE

PAGE 322

BY ONLY MOVING THE SECOND GLASS, POUR THE WATER INTO THE FIFTH GLASS!

TRUE OR FALSE ANSWERS

PAGE 377

1. TRUE – THE FRUIT CAME BEFORE THE COLOUR. BEFORE THE 16TH CENTURY THE COLOUR ORANGE WAS REFERRED TO AS YELLOW-RED.

2. TRUE – THE SEARCH ENGINE BEGAN IN 1996 AND WAS CHANGED TO 'GOOGLE' IN 1997.

3. FALSE – GLUCOSE IS NEEDED FOR FINGERNAILS TO GROW, AND OXYGEN IS REQUIRED FOR HAIR GROWTH – BOTH OF WHICH DO NOT OCCUR IN THE BODY AFTER DEATH.

4. TRUE – 60 SECONDS IN A MINUTE, 60 MINUTES IN A HOUR, 24 HOURS IN A DAY = 86,400!

5. FALSE – WE DO SHARE DNA BUT ONLY 50%.

6. TRUE – TRY IT!